COURAGE

The Fight for Your life

LOUISE L. KALLAWAY

COURAGE...
The Fight for Your life

First published in Australia by Louise L. Kallaway 2025
www.louiselkallaway.com

A catalogue record for this
book is available from the
National Library of Australia

ISBN: 978-0-6459194-7-9 (pbk)

Typesetting and design by Publicious Book Publishing
Published in collaboration with Publicious Book Publishing
www.publicious.com.au

Louise L. Kallaway

I dedicate *'COURAGE'* to my six super special grandchildren:

Ethan, Isabelle, Sophia, Blake, Imogen and Isaac.

I love being part of your lives.

You inspire me to share with you how life works.

ACKNOWLEDGEMENTS

"Suicide is the leading cause of death among young Australians. More than 350 young people aged between 18 to 24 take their own lives every year – this is more than double the number who die on the roads.

For every young person who dies by suicide, there are 100 to 200 more attempts.

Young people may be less likely to attempt suicide if they are resilient and have positive relationships with parents or other adults and close friends."

More triggers for youth suicide can also be found on this site:

www.healthdirect.gov.au.youthsuicide

THE GIST

"Do you believe the Universe created man and all species, then crossed fingers hoping we survived, without structure, without programmed intelligence?

That's not the Universe I know. The Universe has Laws and Divine Order, timing, balance and control.

Night follows day, the four seasons follow each other in logical, sequential order, the mathematical precision of tides, are a few examples of our structured existence.

I believe our lives are structured too, that programmed survival forces help us live a certain way. There's plenty of evidence to support this probability.

Man has evolved, but 'The survival system' we were born into remains unchanged. The 21st Century is being stunted and dumbed down by a survival system, lost to the vastness of time... until now!"

Louise L. Kallaway.

'COURAGE' POWER MENU

DAY 3: STAGE 2 – REBELLION OR SOMETHING MORE?

DAY 4: THE POWER OF YOUR EMOTIONAL LIFE

DAY 5: PERSONAL SUCCESS

HANDOUTS

TO MY READERS

Hello there! A very special welcome. First, congratulations on being the only person like you on Planet Earth. Joining Coach and your five heroic new friends: Grace, Tim, Queenie, Max and Bethy as we venture into the survival system we were all born into, will help you make sense of yourself and your transitioning time zone. You are part of the next generation to run the show, as Max, one of our heroes says. I think you'll love Max. ☺

Be patient, and if you need to, read each chapter a few times to sync with its wisdom. Promise yourself you'll do the exercises with our Heroes and read *'Courage'* from cover to cover, even when it gets a bit heavy. It contains lifesaving and life transforming wisdom... *not available anywhere else.*

Smarter and wiser than 99% of the global population, including your authority figures, is where we are heading as we pioneer uncharted territory and exciting new horizons. Let's win 'the fight' against Youth Suicide.

Here's a beautiful quote to get you started:

"You could search the world, far and wide, to find someone more deserving of your love and affection than yourself, but you'll never find that person. You, yourself, are more deserving of that love than anyone in the Universe."

Buddha.

i

SUMMER SCHOOL

The two-week Summer School for teens and young people is held every year during the Christmas school holidays in the southern hemisphere and during July in the northern hemisphere.

We welcome students from all walks of life from all over the world. It's an opportunity to meet with your age group, explore Universal themes and the many areas in your life that are changing and challenging, particularly peer group and social media pressures, and their conformity expectations.

Our aim is to always create a safe, secure and friendly environment, one where summer school participants are encouraged to speak freely and honestly and learn in a community that has each other's back and welfare at heart, all heading in the same positive direction.

We offer a wide choice of courses ranging from art classes, exercise, music and sporting programs to name a few, but each student must enrol in our most popular and globally acclaimed *'Making Friends with Yourself'* course which runs for 5 consecutive days x 3.5 hours each day. We repeat this course four times in the two weeks and try to keep the numbers to no more than five students in each class. This mandatory course gives students a fabulous understanding of their transitioning time zone and all the forces at work, both visible and invisible, so they are better equipped to handle life in the 21st Century.

DAY 1:

SURVIVAL BASICS

MEET AND GREET

Coach: "Good morning and a big welcome to all five young people, potentially my course Heroes. I am the coach for each of the four compulsory, *'Making Friends with Yourself'* courses on offer at our Summer School each year. Congratulations on being our first group this summer.

I want you to know from the get-go, I am not a psychologist. I am a researcher. I wanted to understand how life works, and to make sense of our lives in the 21ˢᵗ Century. My 30-year research started with the origins of life, but with little documentation available, I pieced together with the help of undeniable evidence today, an ingenious, non-intellectual survival system concerned only with the survival of man and all species. We have been programmed to live a certain way. This system has not changed.

'The survival system' we were born into and the *'Making Friends with Yourself'* Course are both designed to help you survive. I wrote the concept as an original, anti-suicide course aimed at helping young people understand all the pressures and influences they are feeling, not just the obvious pressures at your age, but the invisible pressures you are no doubt feeling from a basic survival perspective.

I've been teaching this course since its inception, and I've met many amazing young people over the years. This Course is franchised world-wide and is now being taught by some of my original students!

To keep it simple, you can call me Coach. I'd like to find out about each of you, your backgrounds and why you've chosen to give up a couple of weeks of your holidays to be here. You may have noticed, we are seated at a round table. *I call this table the Winners' Circle.* Round the table, who'd like to start sharing?"

Five Heroes:

Grace: "I'll start. Hi. My name is Grace. I'm the eldest of four. I have two brothers and a sister. I'm here because my parents think it's important I understand the challenges I'm facing in this transitional stage. I love dancing and competing. My team has won lots of competitions. I'm taking a public speaking class, which I like too."

Tim: "Hi, my name is Tim. I have an older sister. I'm here because I'm finding it difficult to transition into this stage. Taking responsibility for everything that is happening in my life has been challenging for me. My parents wondered if this Course could help me understand what I don't understand and to make 'our' lives easier. I love basketball and I coach a girls' Under 10 basketball team a couple of times a week. We're doing okay in the competitions; we're aiming at the State finals in the next two years."

Queenie: "Hello. I'm Queenie. I have an older brother. I've heard a lot of great stuff about the *'Making Friends with Yourself'* Course. My parents encouraged me to apply and here I am. I'm not exactly sure what's in the Course but I'm willing to give up a couple of weeks of my summer holidays to make my life easier to understand. I'm not outgoing like the other kids in my peer group, but I mix in okay, most of the time. I like reading, drawing and colour, and I love beautiful things."

Max: "Gooday! Call me Max. I have two older sisters. My parents thought this Course could help me understand what's going on in my life. I mix in okay with my peer group, like Queenie, but I like to spend my free time pursuing my interests. My independent behaviour does cause a few problems for others, including my teachers. I love playing in my Heavy Metal band, watching 'escape' movies and reading autobiographies."

Bethy: "Hello. My name is Bethany. Please call me Bethy. I'm an only child. My mum suggested I attend the *'Making Friends with Yourself'* course. She likes to keep up with all the latest stuff... and this course has great reviews. She thought it might help me understand myself and why I have trouble joining in. I like being around people, but I also like my own company; it seems to upset my peer group sometimes. I feel like an outsider, when I don't join in. I wish they'd accept me as I am rather than me change to fit in with them. I like reading non-fiction books and researching. I also like writing short stories. I keep a journal, and I love shopping with my mum."

Coach: "Congratulations to everyone; being here puts you in the Heroes' classification with me. We have a great mix of personalities:

- Grace and Tim are social and competitive. They like dancing and basketball competitions respectively. A couple of 'out there' teens.

- Queenie and Max are more solitary. They mix in okay, but they like to pursue their interests.

- Bethy likes being around people, but she's a bit of a loner. She recognises her solitary behaviour can upset her peer group and it makes her feel like an outsider sometimes.

Before we start, there are a couple of ground rules:

- First, there must be total honesty between us for this course to excel.

- Second, the *'Making Friends with Yourself'* Course is built on respect.

Ridiculing or sniggering when anyone speaks honestly, which is speaking from the heart, will be called out. I want you to understand that speaking from the heart is courageous and it should be respected, no matter your age or stage in life.

One more thing, we learn by repetition, so there'll be plenty of repetition each day. Repetition helps us remember.

Many of us have been touched by suicide, haven't we? It's my job to create a new awareness and a deeper and broader understanding of what you're up against, so you feel safer and not so vulnerable to all the forces going on in your life, both visible and invisible. In other words, smarter and wiser.

There are many reasons why young people commit suicide. We will cover those connected to our survival programming in this Course. Other triggers can be found on the website: www.healthdirect.gov.au.youthsuicide

Understand, my 30-year research and its conclusions conflict and disrupt with traditional viewpoints. There'll be a lot to challenge your thinking, and it may even help you understand from a different perspective any mental health issues you are dealing with.

Most of all, I hope *'Making Friends'* helps you through the maze to a new appreciation of yourself, life and an exciting, inspired future.

Okay, please grab a Course complimentary journal and pen. I encourage you to fill in your journals with everything you learn in this Course that's important to you. It will help jog your memory when you're home.

Clock's ticking... we've got between 8.30 am and midday with a half hour break for five consecutive days to make sense of yourself and your transitioning time zone in the 21st Century.

All ready? Yes? Let's start your journey into smarter and wiser filling in the gaps in the 21st Century with an understanding of our survival programming and time."

SURVIVAL AND THE ORIGINS OF LIFE

Coach: "Life had to start from somewhere, right? Have you thought about survival and the origins of life? You're probably thinking, *"What's the origins of life and survival got to do with me at my age in the 21ˢᵗ Century?"* The answer: *absolutely everything!*

To make sense of your life, understand we were born into a survival system, that cannot be changed. 'The system' was designed to help us survive.

When you feel pressure to fit in and conform with your peer group, know it's 'The system' doing its job, wanting to protect you and to help you survive."

Max: "I have a question. Are you saying that when we feel pressure to fit in and conform with our peer group, it's the same system used when caveman lived? That nothing has changed."

Coach: "Yes, Max, it's the exact same survival system today as it was for caveman. And you're right, nothing has changed.

Understanding life's survival programs and their impact on you today will change your life in powerful and positive ways."

TAKING ON GOLIATH – THE PRIMITIVE SURVIVAL SYSTEM

Coach: "I want to hear from each of you during this course. Let me know I'm not talking to myself. Okay. Ask questions... even if you think they're dumb questions!

We are about to take on Goliath. I call 'The survival system' we were born into Goliath. This system has been forgotten over the vastness of time. It is still helping man, and all species, survive.

You'll soon know how 'The system' works, and you'll feel okay, with or without 'group' approval or anyone's approval. Peer group pressure won't intimidate you so much because you'll know, from a survival perspective, that it's not personal, you are not a victim, they're not picking on you... it's just life doing its job."

Grace: "When you say survival, what do you mean exactly?"

Coach: "Good question Grace.

- Survival is basically eat, drink, sleep and procreate... repeat.

- Caveman children instinctively copied tribal family behaviours they saw frequently. In other words, behaviours were copied and handed down from one generation to the next.

- No words, no thinking! Just mindless, copied, robotic behaviours helping cave people survive.

We inherited this primitive survival system."

Tim: "Are you saying we are living as cavemen?" (Everyone laughing with a few grunts).

Coach ignoring the grunts: "Not exactly Tim. We are not physically living as cavemen, but we are living in the 21ˢᵗ Century with the exact same programs that helped caveman survive. We didn't just land on Planet Earth this Century. We inherited those non-intellectual survival programs that automatically repeat themselves from one generation to the next... forever.

When those survival programs were introduced, did the Universe know that one day we could be living 80 or 90 years with an evolving intellectual brain? Who knows? The point is, when we deny the existence of survival forces, the 21ˢᵗ Century is being stunted and dumbed down by those non-intellectual programs. Any questions? There must be something you are wondering?"

Max: "Can those survival programs ever be turned off? I mean, do we have to understand them before we can evolve?"

Coach: "Great question Max. First, no, the survival programs can never be switched off! Who has that kind of power? And yes, once we understand the survival programs we were all born into and their impact on us in the 21ˢᵗ Century, it gives us an opportunity to evolve a lot faster.

You and previous Course members are living examples of the power of understanding these systems. It will be interesting to see how much further advanced the students who go through my courses will be, compared to their non-educated counterparts. I hope I'm here long enough to witness it!"

Bethy: "Are we the guinea pigs?"

Coach: "I would never think of my Heroes as guinea pigs, Bethy. I like to think of my Course members as smarter and wiser than young people who haven't been lucky enough to be educated into the ways of the world.

Okay, let me set the scene, life in caveman times was about survival, nothing more:

- It was a hostile and dangerous place with dinosaurs, brontosaurus T-rex's, sabre-toothed tigers and the like roaming the countryside, looking for their next feed.

- We lived a very short lifespan compared to today, somewhere between 20 and 35 years… less than half of today's lifespan.

- **Our thinking brain was not operating. We lived an instinctive, repetitive and kneejerk way of reacting to life, helping us escape danger and survive.**

Let's find out how those programs are impacting you today:

- We were born with a powerful Will to Survive. Our sole purpose in life was to survive… nothing more!

- The Will to Survive translated into a 'Need to belong' to a tribe or to a group. **A 'Need to belong' was programmed into our DNA.** Light bulb moment anyone?

- Abandonment was/is a primal fear. How will we survive without someone or a group caring for us?

We were dependent on 'The group' to protect us and to keep us safe. It maintained order with its rules and a conforming 'pack' mentality:

The Universe gave survival power to 'The Group'!

Understand this: A 'Need to belong' to a group applied to every living thing: groups of people, schools of fish, herds of cattle, flocks of birds, packs of wolves. Do you see the wider connection? Who are the groups in your life today?"

Bethy: "Our family, our peer group and any group we belong to."

Coach: "Yes, thank you Bethy. The power of the group still applies to our lives today! Got that? I want to hear it."

Heroes: "Yes, Coach."

Coach: "Everything in 'The survival system' was/is reliant upon a group of some sort to help the species survive... including us!

I'll say it again: 'The survival system' you were born into empowered 'The Group' and a conforming, one rule fits all, 'pack' mentality.

To remain empowered, the group must control you!

Got that Heroes? Nothing has changed... life continues repeating itself from one generation to the next to survive. Basic caveman stuff."

Max: "It's becoming clearer why we *feel* pressure to belong to our peer group, doesn't it guys?"

Coach: "Thank you Max. All on board with why you feel pressure to belong and conform with your peer group?"

Heroes all agreeing: "Yes, Coach."

Coach: "I'm not convinced Heroes! Who'd like to say the same thing in a different way?"

Queenie: "There's a pull to belong to our peer group. It's not only programmed into our DNA, but it's an unconscious survival force."

Coach: "Yes, Queenie... it's an unconscious force! Great understanding! It's the reason why young people *feel* compelled to belong to their peer group. The group, whoever they are, has an agenda! It expects you to knuckle under and conform with them, like it did in caveman times. Its objective is to help you survive. Is this making sense?"

Heroes in unison: "Yes. We get it, Coach!"

Coach: "Excellent! This is a major part of your new understanding – why belonging to your peer group is so powerful at your age. You have been programmed since the origins of life to belong to 'the group'. Your peer group today is exerting pressure on you to belong and to conform with them, as it was programmed to do.

If you questioned your peer group, I doubt they would know why they want you to belong and conform with them. Not too many of your authority figures would know why either.

We'll do more on the survival 'need to belong' as we progress to give you an even deeper appreciation of the whole belonging thing.

A couple more survival programs of a personal nature:

- We were/are born self-protective with our feelings, instincts and senses operating, helping us survive.

- Add fear to our DNA. Fear was/is our constant companion keeping us physically safe and living within its strict boundaries; today, those boundaries are known as our comfort zones.

Heroes, let's acknowledge the programs we were born into that helped us survive. One each:

Queenie: "We were born with a Will to survive."

Grace: "We need to belong to a group."

Tim: "We must conform with the group."

Max: "We were born self-protective with our instincts, feelings and senses operating."

Bethy: "Fear set our boundaries helping us survive."

Coach: "Lucky last, abandonment was/is a primal fear. How will we survive if we're not cared for? Right?

Nothing has changed! It's the same survival system over thousands of years robotically and endlessly repeating itself through the generations, helping us survive. How's everyone feeling about the group and its power?"

Heroes in unison: "You're making sense Coach!"

Coach: "Excellent. Now let's find out how caveman remembered before they could think."

HOW DID CAVEMAN SURVIVE WITHOUT A THINKING BRAIN?

Coach: "One of the key questions in my 30-year research was: how did we survive in caveman times before we could think? Anyone? No?

The subconscious mind was our primitive survival memory.

Has everyone heard of the subconscious mind?"

Heroes: "Yes, Coach."

Coach: "Okay.

- What caveman children saw repeatedly, they copied. Those copied behaviours were hardwired into a child's subconscious mind as basic survival memories. *Basic survival memories stick like glue to our subconscious mind's memory. Those memories were in charge of our survival!*

- **When the subconscious mind recognised a current situation that reminded it of a similar memory, it** *reacted!* **Caveman and their children knew immediately how they felt and what to do.**

- **No thinking, no words… just fast, kneejerk subconscious reactions helping them escape danger and survive.**

There are two time zones operating in 'The survival system' – the childhood time zone with its survival memories is repeated as a present time automatic, kneejerk reaction. No changes, still the same system today.

Any questions?"

Bethy: "Are you saying we still live in that two-time zone system? That what we learnt and saw as little kids we are repeating as we get older?"

Coach: "Yes, Bethy. The system is a two-time zone system. What we learnt and observed as little kids we repeat as a present time reaction. No thinking, just reacting! I know it's heavy-going guys. You must have questions. I need to know you get this."

Tim: "Are you saying everyone is robotic, the same as caveman, when we had no thinking brain?"

Coach: "Yes Tim, the same as caveman! Thank you. The two-time zone system is robotic. One reaction for two different time zones. Copied or learnt generational beliefs, attitudes and behaviours stored in our subconscious mind from childhood, are repeated as a present time survival reaction. This was another ingenious way of life surviving, getting us out of harm's way fast, no thinking.

Reacting **is the key word here. Survival intelligence, by its very nature, is** *instinctive, reactive and repetitive.* **When we couldn't think or didn't have time to think, the subconscious mind with its fast,** *kneejerk reactions* **helped us escape danger and survive. No thinking! Simple caveman stuff!**

This is our basic survival intelligence at work today. Life continuing to react and repeat itself to survive… generational cycles mindlessly repeating themselves.

What about now? What has changed?

- Our intellectual brain is operating

- We live a much longer lifespan

- 'The individual' continues evolving.

Today, survival programs are stunting us and dumbing us down when we deny our programmed existence. More information will be added to these basics over the next four days.

Okay on that note, let's take a well-deserved half hour break. Plenty of refreshments in the kitchen. Your mum's not here, so look behind you and leave the kitchen the way you found it please. Back here by half past."

'THE GROUP' AND ITS INFLUENCE TODAY

Coach: "All refreshed?

Okay, you now understand 'The primitive survival system' gave its power to 'The group' and a conforming, *one rule fits all,* 'Pack' mentality. It's an invisible, unconscious, driven behaviour; one of the most important and powerful survival principles in our lives and yet remarkably, most people deny its existence or don't know this.

When you feel pressure to belong and conform with the group, you now know it's the survival system doing its job! It's not personal. They're not picking on you. You are not a victim. You are now onto 'the group' and its place in survival! You are smarter and wiser. Love that!

As Bethy said earlier, the groups today are your family, your peer group and any group you belong to. Let's include social media groups, clubs, sports teams, bands, dancing teams etc. All of them have a conforming 'Pack' mentality… 'a one rule fits all' policy.

Are you making sense of 'The group' and its influence on your lives?"

Queenie: "Yes, I won't be so intimidated by 'the group' now. Life is making a lot more sense to me. Thanks Coach. What do you think guys?"

Heroes in unison: "Yes. We won't be so intimidated by 'the group' now. Thanks Coach."

Bethy: "Why isn't this taught in schools and where young people hang out? It would save a lot of stress, Coach. May be even save a few lives."

Coach: "Yes, it would Bethy. Thank you. Change of any kind takes time, at least a couple of generations. Life moves slowly. You've got to get past all the nay sayers, all the committees and the hierarchy and then hopefully find people with passion, who believe in the Cause and who want to make constructive, positive changes that will evolve society. Those people are known as 'Lightworkers'."

Tim: "It's almost like the system doesn't want change, putting everything in its way to stop advancement. I don't get it."

Coach: "Thanks Tim. Changes can upset some people, especially those with political and/or financial interests. We'll touch on more reasons why most of us don't like change tomorrow. Okay Tim?"

Tim: "Yes. It will be good to know why change is so difficult. Thanks Coach."

Coach: "Back to the group, pressure to belong and conform with 'the group' doesn't let up! You'll feel pressure all your lives. It's endemic in the system. Why?"

Heroes in unison: "To help us survive."

Coach: "Yes indeed! I also want you to know: 'The group' will never care for you like it cares for itself; it will never share its power and it's not interested in the individual. The individual was given no power in 'The survival system'!

Let's find out what's happening in your lives now:

You are swapping alliances from your *'childhood tribal family group'* for survival, to your *'peer group/your generation'* for support and acceptance to feel okay about yourselves, but...

There's a catch, a BIG catch:

Handing responsibility for your approval over to a group (or to anyone) to feel okay about yourself *gives them your power* and puts you in vulnerable territory.

Who'd like to paraphrase what I just said? Anyone?"

Grace: "I'll try. When you hand responsibility for your approval over to a group or to anyone, you give them your power, making you vulnerable."

Coach: "Yes Grace! Thank you. Repeat Grace's words Heroes and say it like you mean it."

Heroes raising their voices: "When you hand responsibility for your approval over to a group or to anyone, you give them your power, making you vulnerable!"

Coach: "Clever, isn't it? What happens if you defy the group and decide not to fit in and conform?"

Bethy: "You risk being rejected."

Coach: "That's right! Bethy.

You risk being rejected or excluded! Got that Heroes? In fact, expect to be rejected or excluded if you can't, don't or choose not to fit in and conform with the group! I'll say it again: It's not personal! You're not a victim! They're not picking on you! The threat of rejection or exclusion is how they intimidate everyone! It's caveman's programming, alive and well in the 21st Century!

Now, think about this: the group is all about itself, its power and its control. From a survival perspective, 'The group' cares jack about the individual! ☺ Got that Heroes? Let me hear from someone."

Tim: "The individual means jack to the group; it's all about group power. Everyone huddled in the group for protection and survival in caveman times. The individual was not a thing back then."

Coach: "Yes, Tim. Thank you. It was all about group power. The Universe gave survival power to the group. The individual was not a thought back then.

Now, think about this: would you give up your life for a group, that from a survival perspective, doesn't care jack about the individual. Are they worth it? What do you think Heroes?"

Max: "I've never thought about it like that. I wouldn't give up my life because I wasn't accepted by my peer group or any group or anyone for that matter or if I wanted to be more independent! What do you think guys?"

Heroes in unison shouting: "No way!"

Coach: "Great to hear Heroes!

A major power base throughout your life will always be: self-acceptance above the need for group acceptance.

Here's affirmation #1 Heroes:

"It's good to feel my power and it's great to own my power!"

What's your #1 affirmation Heroes? Say it like you mean it!"

Heroes shouting: "It's good to feel my power and it's great to own my power!"

Coach: "One more thing: should you hit a downward spiral, try saying this to yourself:

"No matter how much trouble I'm in,
how 'different', desperate or unsupported I feel,
I will get through this. This is a phase, and I will be okay."

That is your personal power talking to you Heroes.

Know this too: there is nothing wrong with you! The system is rigged against the individual owning power. It was the group in the survival system who called the shots. This shift in your understanding at your age has the potential to be life changing.

Why is 'the system' rigged against the individual? Anyone?"

Queenie: "The Universe gave power to the group to help us survive."

Coach: "Yes, Queenie. Thank you. The Universe gave power to the group to help us survive.

Here's affirmation #2 and again, say it like you mean it!

I will not give up my life for anyone or a group.
I have the courage to walk away."

Heroes shouting: "I will not give up my life for anyone or a group. I have the courage to walk away."

Coach: "Excellent... hang onto those words Heroes! Speaking of courage, has anyone heard of *Jonathan Livingstone Seagull*?"

Queenie: "Yes. He was an independent seagull who liked to soar high above the flock. The other birds talked about him behind his back trying to make him look and feel foolish, basically to make him conform, but it didn't work. He was the one having all the fun, making his life incredibly satisfying, as he challenged himself, soaring higher every day, breaking the group's conformity rules and making new records for himself."

Coach: "Brilliant critique Queenie! *Jonathan Livingstone Seagull* was an independent bird! While all the other seagulls were bickering among themselves and talking about him disparagingly, he was up there having all the fun. He would not allow the flock to pressure him into living a mediocre life with them. Does that sound like something you'd be interested in reading? I hope so. Previous course heroes have loved Jonathan, and a few have even modelled their lives on his courage! ☺

By the way, independent does not mean rebellious!

It's a tiny book, filled with wisdom and it won't take long to read. Do yourself a big favour... buy yourself a copy, borrow it from your local library, or ask for a copy as a birthday or Christmas gift. Richard Bach (1936 -) is the author, *'Jonathan Livingstone Seagull'* is the name of the book, first published in 1970. Still selling today.... I know, because I recently bought a copy for Ethan, my eldest grandchild. He loved Jonathan's independence.

Here's another individual. Has everyone heard of Steve Jobs?"

Heroes in unison: "Apple computers."

Coach: "Yes. The late Steve Jobs (1955-2011) was the co-founder of Apple computers. Steve Jobs had no formal tertiary qualifications; he had a vision that personal computers could be in every home globally. He liked to spend time on his own romancing his vision; he also liked to hang out with society's alternatives, rebels, misfits, outsiders, generally people who were considered 'different'. He thought they were interesting. In fact, Jobs mostly hired society's alternatives to help fulfill his vision.

He named Apple's slogan: 'Think different.' 'Think different' changed the world... forever.

Now let's talk about feeling 'different' and pressure to conform."

FEELING 'DIFFERENT' & PRESSURE TO CONFORM

Coach: "Who has felt group pressure? Maybe from your peer group or social media. Any kind of group pressure? How did you feel? Anyone?"

Queenie: "I've felt group pressure. I don't always conform, but on that occasion, I felt like there was something wrong with me, that I was a misfit. It was embarrassing. I'll never forget it."

Coach: "Thank you for being our Hero, Queenie. Spoken from the heart. Group pressure to conform had you feeling like there was something wrong with you, a misfit. Anyone else?"

Max: "Me too. I've felt peer pressure to conform. It does feel like you're some kind of outsider, a misfit. It left a few scars. You don't forget the experience."

Coach: "Thanks Max. Interesting. Queenie and Max are the two teens among us who are more solitary, and a little more independent. They like their own space, and they don't always fit in and conform with their peer group. Bethy, any thoughts?"

Bethy: "That's exactly how I've been feeling all my life. I've often felt alone and sometimes I think I must be weird. I know my mum worries about it. I've never felt I could join in like the other kids in my peer group... it wasn't me. No matter how hard I tried, I didn't fit in and I didn't feel comfortable belonging to any group. Sometimes I wish I could be like them, but I'm not."

Coach: "Thank you Bethy and all the Heroes in this Course... I love your honesty.

Okay, now let's look at 'feeling different' and the pressure to conform.

Being 'different' is not only scary for you, I want you to understand, 'different' is also scary for 'the group'. They don't want you to be different; they want *everyone* in the group to think the same, dress the same, look the same, behave the same or how will they control you?

This is nothing more than the primitive survival system at work in the 21st Century. Groups... flocks, herds, packs... whoever they are, pressure mankind and all species to conform! Not just children, adolescents, teens and young people, but throughout our lives. We've been conditioned to believe, with the help of our programming, that we must belong to a group. Everyone and every species, even seagulls! That's how we've survived for thousands of years. The groups' job is to help us survive with its strength in numbers, 'conform or risk rejection' mentality.

We give up our power to belong and conform with the group, so we are not rejected. But, handing responsibility for your approval over to someone or to a group to feel okay about yourself, *gives them your power*. It puts you in vulnerable territory! I want to really drive this point home."

Max: "That is making so much sense Coach! What you are saying is: we are trading our independence as an individual to belong to a group."

Coach: "Excellent understanding Max! Everyone got that?

There is always a trade-off when we make a choice.

To belong or not to belong, is a perfect example. If you decide to belong to a group, then you will conform with their rules or risk rejection. You are trading your independence as an individual to belong to the group. See how it works? All actions have consequences, including non-actions.

COURAGE... SURVIVAL BASICS

When things get tough or when the group (whoever they are) starts their campaign to make you conform, and you choose not to, know you are making a choice that has consequences. Just like *Jonathan Livingstone Seagull* made his choice to be independent and fly on his own. All on-board with this?"

Heroes: "Yes Coach. We get it!"

Coach: "Good to know. Now…

Let's check out how the stigma of 'different' came into our lives:

We've all been conditioned to think the same, dress the same, behave the same and conform with the groups, the family group and the little kids' play groups, kindergarten etc. We learnt as little kids that 'different' is a difficult fit. 'Different' is hard on young people to feel okay about themselves too.

Feeling 'different', not fitting in, not conforming with the group, feeling like an outsider or a misfit, and the ultimate feeling of rejection by 'The group', is undeniably emotionally painful for not just your age, but for all of us. Those feelings, as uncomfortable and as embarrassing as they are, are painful but they won't kill you! Got that?"

Heroes: "Yes, Coach."

Coach: "You have all the power when it comes to life or death, it's your choice. And I can tell you… rejection by the group is not worth taking your life, especially as I said earlier, most likely members of the group don't even know why they want you to fit in and conform with them. All they know is, you should… it's an expectation. Why is it expected?"

Bethy: "Belonging to and conforming with 'the group' is programmed into our DNA."

Coach: "Yes, Bethy, thank you. Belonging to and conforming with 'the group' is a survival program. It's built into our DNA.

Promise me Heroes, promise yourself and everyone who cares for you... that if you feel intimidated by peer group pressure, no matter who the group is, know it's the survival system doing its job! It's not personal! They're not picking on you! You are not a victim! They treat everyone who doesn't fit in, who is 'different' and who doesn't conform with them... the same.

Life is a precious gift. You are an individual and there will never be anyone else like you... ever again. You have no idea how amazing you are and how great you can be, or how many exciting things lay ahead for you. Don't give up on yourself, don't waste your talents and please don't take your life. There are organisations like Headspace ready to listen and to help you with your feelings or your situation 24/7.

You are now awake to the system we were all born into that demands you fit in and conform to survive! You decide whether you want to, don't want to, can't or won't fit in and conform, all the time, sometimes or never. It's up to you and remember, choices have consequences; it will take courage to act on those choices. You are the powerful one now.

We'll learn more about choices and how to handle rejection tomorrow.

Remember your course affirmations? Repeat them with me. Nice and loud.

Coach & Heroes in unison:

"It's good to feel my power and it's great to own my power!
I will not give up my life for anyone or a group.
I have the courage to walk away."

Coach: "Excellent, Heroes! I want you to be aware of something else: the 'Need to belong' and conform with 'the group' continues throughout your lives. Any thoughts?"

Max: "So, belonging to and conforming with the group continues, ganging-up on us throughout our lives helping us survive. Right?"

Coach: "I'd never thought of it as 'ganging up' Max. ☺ Great connection! Yes, that's exactly what's happening. The Universe is ganging up on you, helping you survive. It means no harm, it's a form of protection, so all species will be safe and survive with the help of the group and its conforming 'pack' mentality."

Bethy: "So, we're programmed to believe we must belong to a group all our lives."

Coach: "Yes, Bethy. That's exactly what our survival programming has us all believing... all our lives. It doesn't let up! Even in midlife, if we decide to forge an independent path rather than conform with group expectations, it is seen as a 'Midlife crisis' rather than the maturing adult simply outgrowing his conditioning and fulfilling his maturing needs and potential like *Jonathan Livingstone Seagull* and Steve Jobs. Plenty to think about. Sorry guys, we're out of time. Your homework: write in Heroes' Notes what you learnt today that has you feeling less intimidated by 'the group' and more empowered."

Also, choose your confidant, someone you would talk to if you felt intimidated or pressured by anyone or a group, or if you were rejected or excluded by your peer group.

We'll start tomorrow with revision of today's power points, and we'll investigate Stage 1 of your life, childhood. There'll also be an opportunity to test one of your subconscious reactions in Day 2. Very exciting.

Enjoy your afternoon. See you here at 8.30 am sharp tomorrow."

HEROES' NOTES

THE NEED TO BELONG AND GROUP CONFORMITY

The Universe gave survival power to 'The group' and a conforming 'Pack' mentality.

How will this new understanding of 'the group' (whoever they are) help you feel less intimidated by 'group' pressure to conform?

....

....

....

....

List some ways you feel more empowered:

....

....

....

....

Who would you speak to if you were pressured or rejected by a group?

....

....

....

DAY 2:

CHILDHOOD & SURVIVAL PROGRAMS

REVISION AND INTRODUCTION

Coach: "Good morning, Heroes. Ready for another big day? Yes? Let's revise yesterday's session and the basic key points of our programmed lives. Round the winners' circle... who'd like to start?"

Queenie: "I'll start. We were born with a Will to survive."

Max: "We were born self-protective with our instincts, feelings and senses all operating."

Bethy: "Fear set our boundaries and helped us survive."

Grace: "To survive, we needed to belong to a group."

Tim: "We needed to conform with the group."

Coach: "That's five Heroes. Anyone remember the sixth program?

Tim: "Was it, abandonment is a primal fear?"

Coach: "Yes, Tim! Thank you. Excellent work Heroes! ☺ And there are two time zones operating in the survival system and in our lives today. Our subconscious mind repeats learnt childhood beliefs, attitudes and behaviours in present time, as one fast, automatic, kneejerk reaction! No thinking! Caveman stuff!

Does anyone know who identified this two-time zone behaviour? No? It was Aristotle. Have you heard of him?"

Heroes: "Not sure."

Coach: "Aristotle was an ancient Greek philosopher, C. 384 B.C. – 322 B.C. He said:

"Give me a child until he is seven and I will show you the man."

This is basic to your understanding Heroes. It's not just the adult repeating childhood beliefs, attitudes and copied behaviours; it applies to all ages including adolescents, teenagers and young people, automatically repeating what they learnt and observed as little kids.

No thinking! *Reacting* is the key word here. Survival intelligence, is, by its very nature, *instinctive, repetitive and reactive*. It's how and why generational cycles continue repeating themselves. Who'd like to say this in a different way?"

Bethy: "What we learnt and saw as little kids is stored in our subconscious mind and is repeated when a similar situation is happening in present time."

Coach: "Yes. Thank you, Bethy. Everyone got this."

Heroes: "Yes. Got it Coach!"

Coach: "Great! Did everyone choose a confidant? A person you would speak to if you felt pressured or rejected by 'the group' or an individual (including a romantic rejection)?"

Heroes in unison: "Yes, Coach."

Coach: "Excellent Heroes. We'll do more on rejection later this morning and in the days ahead.

Let's find out about Stage 1: your Childhood."

CHILDHOOD: STAGE 1 OF YOUR DEVELOPMENT

Coach: "We've just discussed the two-time zone system we were born into. Now I'd like to show you, how the two-time zone system works in our lives today.

Again, please ask questions so I know you are connecting. Don't be afraid to speak up. By speaking up, you'll encourage your new friends to speak up.

Okay, let's make sense of yourself today. Childhood is Stage 1 in your development. The little kid in you is known colloquially as your inner child. I like to call the little kid in us, our backseat driver. Do you know what a backseat driver means?"

Max: "Yes. You're behind the steering wheel but someone in the backseat is telling you how to drive, where to go, and how fast."

Coach: "Yes, Max. You're behind the steering wheel, but someone in the backseat is giving you directions and instructions which in this case is your inner child. Let's find out how the backseat driver works in our lives today.

As a baby and a little kid, you were conditioned into the ways of the world. Your inner child forms your beliefs, attitudes and behaviours in the first seven years (your survival foundations) mostly copied from the previous generation. The little kid in you doesn't know he is collecting this data and that his survival beliefs, attitudes and copied behaviours are being hardwired like glue into your subconscious mind's memory for future ready reference, helping you survive.

We talked yesterday and again this morning about how survival beliefs, attitudes and copied behaviours learnt in childhood continue repeating themselves. When the subconscious mind identifies what is happening now that is like a memory from the past, that survival memory will be repeated as a present time reaction. Any questions?"

Tim: "Just confirming, this is how and why we are like robots. We don't think, we react and repeat. Right?"

Coach: "Yes Tim. Thank you. That is exactly how and why we become like robots, on 'auto-pilot'. We unconsciously repeat our childhood beliefs, attitudes and behaviours, the same as caveman thousands of years ago.

The first seven years of our lives today is comparable to caveman times. Neither caveman children nor today's children were/are capable of thinking. The little kid in you watched and copied the beliefs, attitudes and behaviours he saw frequently from the previous generation, exactly as caveman children did in those times. Both eras stored this survival data in their subconscious minds."

Grace: "Coach, are you saying nothing has changed, that the first seven years of our lives today was the same program for caveman too?"

Coach: "Yes. Thank you, Grace. The first seven years is when we were programmed to copy the previous generation's beliefs, attitudes and behaviours to help us survive. What we learnt and observed were/are hardwired and stored in our subconscious minds, sticking like glue, and becoming our fast, subconscious kneejerk reactions potentially for the rest of our lives. All clear on this?"

Bethy: "So the first seven years establishes our take on life, right? If we had a hard time or if we saw repeated violence or if we had an easy time, then that becomes our attitude to life. Is that what you're saying?"

Coach: "Getting a bit heavy now Bethy, but yes, that's how important the first seven years is in our lives. It sets up our attitudes, our feelings about ourselves etc. This is invaluable information if you have children of your own someday. You, as the parent, have the power to decide how a child will feel about itself and its attitude to life. Smarter and wiser again guys! How's everyone going with this?"

Heroes: "Good Coach." (Nodding).

Coach: "Your survival foundations from the first seven years forms your Childhood Model, the blueprint for how the literal little kid in you believes life is supposed to be. What does literal mean? Anyone?"

Queenie: "I think literal means accepting what we hear, see and feel as the truth, without question?"

Coach: "Yes Queenie. Thank you. It's the inner child trusting, believing and accepting everything it hears, sees and feels at face value, without question. It trusts its carers and the VIPs in its life.

Does anyone know why a child is literal, that is, why it accepts everything at face value?"

Tim: "Because it's too young to think."

Coach: "Yes Tim… your inner child's brain is not sufficiently developed to think before the age of seven. It can't reason, question or discriminate for example."

Grace: "Can I query you on something please Coach?"

Coach: "Yes Grace, of course."

Grace: "I am the eldest of four and I've heard my sister and both brothers say 'why'… many times."

Coach: "Oh, yes. Well picked up Grace. 'Why' is asked many times by little kids, isn't it? 'Why' means their intellectual brain is developing. They are not asking why we believe something or arguing with our point of view. They are asking a simple question like, "Why are there rainbows?" But, how much of our explanation do they really understand?"

Grace: "So, little kids 'why' questions are simple and basic. They're not debating what we said. That makes sense. Thanks, Coach."

Coach: "You're very welcome, Grace. Now let's quickly run through Stage 1 of your development:

- In the first seven years, your inner child establishes its survival foundations… its beliefs, attitudes, and copied generational behaviours and they are stored like glue in your subconscious mind.

- Those survival foundations are called the Childhood Model of life.

- When your subconscious mind recognises a belief, an attitude, a behaviour or a situation happening in present time that reminds it of a survival foundation, your subconscious mind *reacts and repeats that survival memory.*

- No thinking! You've been programmed to react and repeat your survival foundations automatically. You are on autopilot.

That's how we've survived for thousands of years. It's just life reacting and repeating itself over and over through the generations to survive. Got this?"

Heroes talking among themselves: "Yep. We've got this Coach!"

Coach: "Okay. Let's add another layer."

YOUR CHILDHOOD BRAIN

Coach: "Today in the first seven years, your intellectual left-side brain is in its rudimentary stages of development and does not contribute to your Childhood Model. The same as in primitive times when there was no intellect. All the work is done by the right-side, the feeling side of your brain in the first seven years. Wow! Doesn't that knock you out guys?"

Max: "Coach, are you saying that we are reacting to a literal Childhood Model, potentially all our lives, that has no intellectual input."

Coach: "Yes, Max. The Childhood Model has no intellectual input. A literal child's version of life is running all our stages in life when we deny our programmed existence. Crazy! Right?"

Queenie: "It's scary, Coach."

Coach: "It sure is scary, Queenie.

Did you know your feelings have a direct and harmonious relationship with your subconscious mind. Your subconscious mind does not recognise your intellect... ever! It works exclusively with your feelings, all your life, especially your repetitive, emotionally intense feelings.

The beginning of the difference between caveman times and us today is around seven years old, our left-side intellectual brain has developed enough to think. TOO LATE! It's our inner child's *literal* Childhood Model that reminds us what to do, what we believe and how we feel, repeating itself and reacting, like it did in primitive times, potentially for the rest of our lives. We are now on 'autopilot' with most people in the world.

You are now years ahead in your understanding of life! Any questions?"

Max: "Are you saying we know more than our parents and our teachers?"

Coach: "Put it this way Max, if your parents and/or your teachers are in denial about life's survival forces, then the answer is yes! Today's intellectual logic and our ego find it difficult to accept, in fact, think it's improbable, even fanciful, that the two-time system is still dictating their lives today. They think, *"Give me a child until he is seven and I will show you the man"* has no relevance in the 21st Century.

What's your #1 affirmation Heroes?"

Heroes together: "It's good to feel my power and it's great to own my power."

Coach: "Sure is! Before we get into the Childhood Model, I'd like to show you how and why you can't be like anyone else! More conclusive power!"

CHILDHOOD 'WORLD OF DIFFERENCES'

Coach: "To make even more sense of why we are all different, let's start with your childhood 'world of differences'. Let's focus on the tribal family. Make notes, if you like:

- Where in the sequence of siblings were you born? Were you the first child, second, third or fourth child? The sequence of your birth has significant differences within each family structure. For example, the eldest child is often expected to be 'responsible' or the one who sets the example for the younger kids in the family.

- Were you an only child or a stepchild?

- Did you have two-parents caring for you or were you born into a one parent family?

- Did your grandparents play an active role in your upbringing?

- Were there any issues related to addiction or mental health?

- Did one or both your parents work? Part time or full time? Did they work for someone or were they self-employed?

- Was there an expectation you would follow in the family business?

You can see from these simple family questions, how different we all are.

Add to your answers, all the rules, standards and generational beliefs at the time, your personality and the expectations of your tribal family, it's obvious we can never be the same.

As different as we all are, we've been brought up to fit in and conform with the family group, the play group, kindergarten etc. Our conditioning has us believing 'different' is not good, it's not acceptable.

By the time children go to school, they have learnt that 'different' is a stigma and 'different' is not tolerated by 'the group' and society generally. Different is hard on children emotionally. Every child wants to assimilate and blend in with their friends and later adolescents, teens and young people like to blend in with their peer groups too. They want to feel accepted and supported and not be put in the spotlight. Any comments?"

Max: "You're saying it's okay to feel different because we are different! Every person is unique, and we're learning that it's okay to be an individual, if we have the courage. Pretty powerful stuff. I'm loving this... I'll write some lyrics and set them to heavy metal music! Thanks Coach."

Heroes: "Yeah! We're loving this too. Thanks Coach."

Tim: "A Heavy Metal band and you write lyrics too Max? You are my Hero!"

Queenie: "Can I say something that might upset you Coach?"

Coach: "Upset me? Mmm ...interesting! What might upset me, Queenie?"

Queenie: "My parents deny they have an inner child. I've heard them talking. They think it's BS."

Coach: "Very brave of you to say so, Queenie. Don't worry... I get plenty of deniers. Who else would like to give us an opinion?"

Tim: "Same with my family Coach."

Bethy: "My mum is open to new information. She said open your mind and see where it takes you."

Max: "I don't know much about it, but it all sounds logical to me. I've heard myself sound like my dad, same tone in my voice, and same expression on my face, taking on their attitudes. Pretty scary stuff guys! Is that what I'm going to look like at his age too!"

Coach: "Tone of voice and facial expression. Well picked up Max. Grace. How about you?"

Grace: "I'm okay with what I'm learning so far Coach. This course has been applauded, and it's been franchised around the world, so it must have merit. I want to make sense of my life, and *I want something to believe in.*"

Coach: "Okay. We've a good variety of thoughts. Let's see if today's session can convert everyone to believing they have an inner child. To do this, let's find out what kind of things would be in your literal Childhood Model."

THE BLUEPRINT: YOUR CHILDHOOD MODEL OF LIFE

Coach: "What do you think might be in a child's model of life? Let's go round the winners' circle starting with Queenie."

Queenie: "I'm guessing, beliefs about yourself and your potential."

Max: "Coping and copied behaviours."

Bethy: "All the rules, expectations and the standards we were conditioned to believe."

Grace: "The 'need to belong' and conform."

Tim: "Generational attitudes and values."

Queenie: "Criticisms and compliments."

Coach: "Great answers Heroes! There's more of course but I can see you have a good grasp on the kind of things you've been conditioned to believe in the first seven years. Well done!

Your childhood beliefs, whatever they are, have the power to become your successes or your failures, expanding your possibilities or holding you back. Again, can you see how important the first seven years is from a whole of life perspective? Any questions?"

Grace: "Are you saying we can never change childhood beliefs?"

Coach: "Fab question Grace. No, not exactly. What I'm saying is people who deny life's programmed survival forces, especially the two-time zone system we were all born into, become stuck in their reactive and repetitive subconscious childhood beliefs, attitudes and behaviours, especially in midlife, and wonder why they feel 'stuck' and powerless. It goes back to the two time zones:

"Give me a child until he is seven and I will show you the man."

Everyone okay with this? (No comments). Let me bring this concept into your time zone. The things you were conditioned to believe in childhood such as you can't be 'different', you need to fit in and conform with the group 'stick like glue' in your subconscious and make it difficult for adolescents, teenagers and young people to think that 'different', not fitting in and not conforming is okay. One belief, two time zones, remember. Does that help your understanding?"

Heroes in unison: "Yes Coach. We're on autopilot."

Coach: "Alright! Another major point is that the little kid in you will always remain in his childhood. He doesn't grow up… ever! You will always be the child too until you realise the system we were born into has two-time zones and one subconscious reaction for both time zones.

You are about to form a powerful alliance with your inner child to help make sense of your life.

This empowering information puts you miles ahead of previous generations. Goliath, the primitive survival system, is folding under our pressure Heroes! ☺ Love this! You are paving the way for future generations. Let's expose more of life's secrets."

DIFFERENT PERSPECTIVES BETWEEN TIME ZONES

Coach: "Let's find out what a difference time makes between your literal childhood interpretations and your age. Let's focus on a few subjects from your Childhood Model that would most likely be affecting you now:

- No understanding of time or change

- No signs of independence

- No alternative choices

- No input into your childhood image

- The serious, humourless, personal world of a child

- Fear and its comfort zones.

Let's start with:

No understanding of time or change:

The Childhood Model contains little, if any, reference to time or change. As far as your 'backseat driver' is concerned, everything he is learning will remain the same, forever. Permanence gives your inner child a sense of security and certainty. In other words, the little kid in you doesn't like change!

How do you think that might be impacting you today?"

Queenie: "We are basically robots; our inner child's beliefs about time and change would be coming through our subconscious mind as the same reaction. We like feeling secure and we like certainty; we don't like change either."

Coach: "Wow! You just blitzed time and change Queenie! What a fabulous answer! Applause for Queenie, everyone. Hooray! ☺☺☺☺☺ The little kid's already formed view that he doesn't like change because he wants to feel secure, is exactly our reaction! We like certainty too, don't we? And we don't like change! The little kid in you sets the agenda. We follow like robots… until now! How about you Tim? Did that answer your question about change from yesterday?"

Tim: "Yes, Coach. A light bulb moment for me! We are living our childhood over again, when we don't understand or we deny the survival system. Thanks Coach."

Coach: "You're very welcome, Tim. Everyone okay with this?"

Heroes: "All good Coach."

Coach: "Let's do another one:

No alternative choices:

The little kid in you lived in a yes-or-no, right-or-wrong, can-or-can't, black-or-white, either/or world which felt to your inner child that it had no alternative choices. Remember, your inner child's brain can't reason or discriminate."

Max: "I'll compare this one Coach. Today, we can introduce 'grey' into a child's black-or-white position to give us alternative choices. We can add maybe to an either/or situation, or we can negotiate a better deal than just this way or that. It's a gutsy move, I know, but we can be in charge of alternative choices… if we have the courage."

Coach: "Yes Max. You smashed it! We can be in charge of alternative choices… if we have the courage! Everyone okay with this?"

Heroes chatting between themselves: "Yes, it's exciting! We're on-board Coach!"

Coach: "Excellent, Heroes. Let's do another one:

No signs of independence:

There are no signs of independence in the Childhood Model. Your inner child had no responsibility for itself – your carers and other VIPs were responsible for you and did most things for you.

Can you see how this might be creating problems in your life today?"

Tim: "Everyone did everything for us when we were little kids. We've never learnt any kind of independence like being responsible for ourselves, but suddenly our authority figures at our age are expecting us to do something we've never learnt to do... self-responsibility is new to us. I really get this! This is where my problem with self-responsibility has its beginnings. Wow! Another light bulb moment. Thanks Coach!"

Coach: "You're very welcome, Tim. Excellent understanding."

Heroes in unison: "We're living our childhood all over again Coach!"

Coach: "Yes you are! And throughout your life... if you're in denial! We're on a roll Heroes, there's more.

No input into your childhood image:

This is another big one. Your inner child's feelings about himself and his identity, sense of importance, self-esteem, value and self-worth were all formed from the feedback he was receiving.

He instinctively interpreted the feedback by how others reacted to him. Anyone want to have a go at this?"

Queenie: "If we don't understand the two-time zones, Coach, we think of ourselves from our inner child's interpretation to validate who we believe we are today. My childhood image must be affecting me. I've often thought I'm not good enough or as good as the other kids. My career choices and potential would be impacted too. This is a light bulb moment for me."

Coach: "I'll ask you more about your 'not enough' feelings tomorrow, Queenie, but well done to figure all that out. Yes. Positive or negative, your childhood image does impact your feelings about yourself, possibly your career choices and your potential. So, our image needs updating to suit who we are today, rather than your 'backseat driver' having all the say. You have more life experience now compared to when you were 4 years old or 7 years old. Everyone okay with this?"

Heroes excitedly: 'Yes, Coach."

Coach: "We'll update your image in Day 5.

There's a movie I'd like to draw to your attention that is particularly relevant to what you are learning now. It was released in 1997. The movie is called, *'Goodwill Hunting'*. It stars Matt Damon and the late and great Robin Williams (1951–2014). Anyone heard of *Goodwill Hunting?*"

Max and Bethy: "Yes Coach. Matt Damon was a janitor, wasn't he?"

Coach: "Yes. Matt Damon was a janitor in the movie and Robin Williams was his psychiatrist. The point of watching this movie, even a couple of times, is to help you understand that everyone's childhood experiences continue affecting us years later in current time.

Robin Williams' words, *"It's not your fault"* repeated over and over to Matt Damon reduced Damon to tears, getting through his defences so he could see how his childhood beliefs had been affecting his current behaviour and thinking. He was finally able to accept his genius mathematical potential and allow his romantic relationship to progress. Brilliant movie Heroes!

'Goodwill Hunting' won an academy award for best actor in a supporting role. Please find time to watch it, if you haven't already. It's very revealing. Ben Affleck and Matt Damon wrote the script. Fabulous story from two wonderfully talented young men. They obviously understood what you are learning this week.

Let's do another time zone difference.

The serious, humourless, personal world of a child:

Coming from a little kid's perspective, life is personal and serious. How can it not be? Your inner child's world was centred around itself with its 'need to belong', total dependence on your carers, fear, and security issues. I'll add here, your inner child has no humour about itself. Previous course members have picked me up on a child being humourless until I explain that a child will laugh at other kids falling over, for example, but *never* when he falls over. The little kid in you sees no humour about himself, taking everything that happens to him and his life, personally and seriously.

Is your life 'personal' and serious? Do you lack a sense of humour about yourself too? I'm trying to help my Heroes see that your inner child sets the standard and now it's your job throughout your lives to be more aware and flexible. How do you feel about this?"

Bethy: "So, our seriousness and personalising everything in our lives and our lack of humour about ourselves all starts in our childhood. Are you saying it's also connected to survival?"

Coach: "Terrific assessment and so sensitive too Bethy. Thank you. Does everyone get what Bethy just said? Taking ourselves and our lives seriously and personalising everything, with no humour about ourselves, has its origins in childhood. I believe it *is* connected to our survival. We were born self-protective, remember? The Universe wants us to take the gift of life seriously. *If we were not born self-protective, do you think we would have survived?*"

Queenie: "Probably not."

Coach: "That's right Queenie…probably not. Let's do the lucky last and then we'll take our break.

Fear and comfort zones:

You now know, fear was built into our DNA, with its *'fight or flight'* adrenaline reactions to help us stay safe and survive. Fear is your inner child's comfort zone dictator. Every time your inner child felt fear, he retreated. Fear prepares you for physical danger (as it did in primitive times in a hostile environment), but the little kid in you doesn't know this and can't make such a distinction. Fear sees itself as your protector. It wants to remain the Master of your life helping you survive… that's its job!

I like to think of fear as our personal bodyguard.

Fear worries about you if it thinks you'll hurt yourself or if you're putting yourself at risk or in danger, or if you are thinking about moving into uncharted territory like standing up for yourself. That's why you get butterflies, feel

anxious or stressed or have an adrenaline reaction! Does that interpretation help you see fear as your friend, protecting you and looking after you?"

Heroes in unison nodding: "A personal bodyguard is a great idea Coach."

Coach: "Are you feeling more empowered as you learn about your programmed life? Anyone with a comment?"

Tim: "I had no idea how much our lives were/are programmed. My life is making a lot more sense now, Coach. I know I don't have to follow the leader. I like belonging to my peer group and my basketball team. It's my choice. I also understand it would be a gutsy move not to conform, as Max said. How do you feel Grace?"

Grace: "I feel the same. I've always liked going along with the group. I like to be social, so it's been easy for me to comply. Standing up to my peer group is something I've never done. It would be a courageous move. Thanks Coach. I never realised how difficult it must be for people who aren't social. I feel empathy and compassion for them now."

Coach: "Empathy and compassion for your fellow man, Grace. Nice touch. Give Tim and Grace a cheer for seeing a 'less social' point of view. Hooray! ☺☺☺☺☺ Do you all feel the same or does anyone have a different perspective about standing up to your peer group?"

Bethy: "I can see Tim and Grace's position. If you've never stepped away from 'the group', it would be a scary thing to do. As I've said before, I've never felt that I fitted in, and I've never conformed with any group. I know I'm different and I'm okay with that. The interesting thing is I don't feel their pressure like I used to.

The group seems okay accepting that I'm a bit of a loner. There's a mutual respect. I think it comes down to setting the standard and the boundaries that suit us as individuals. When we feel strongly about something, we have the option of choices."

Coach: "I'm impressed. Two fabulously different perspectives. Anyone got another point of view?"

Queenie: "I generally don't have trouble fitting in and conforming if it feels right for me, but at other times, if I feel strongly enough about something, I sit that one out. I like my own space, and I like to think about things before I blindly follow to stay 'in' with the crowd. It takes courage to step away. Growing up shouldn't be this hard!"

Coach: "Bravo Queenie. I agree, growing up shouldn't be this hard! Max, what do you think?"

Max: "I'm like Queenie, I go along with the group sometimes, but I also like my own space. The group would still prefer 'we' knuckle under and conform, but it seems to have accepted the individual in us if we show we are not scared to go our own way sometimes. I agree with Queenie that it comes down to what we *feel* comfortable with and what we *feel* strongly about. Then it's part of the self-responsibility thing to make a decision that *feels* right for us, no matter the opinion of others. I can see Grace and Tim's viewpoints and Bethy's too."

Coach: "Off the charts, guys!

What deniers don't understand and what makes you smarter and wiser Heroes, is that you know we live in a two-time zone, one reaction system. Our fast, automatic reactions lock us into the Childhood Model, especially fitting in and conforming, until we understand how life and 'the survival system' works.

One more thing: Without your new understanding, Childhood Model beliefs can have us all thinking… that, is all we are, and this, is all we can be, holding us back and frustrating us, especially as we get older. As I've said countless times, it's just life endlessly repeating itself, one generation after the next, helping us survive.

We are disrupting the pattern: You now know you have choices.

Okay, time for our 30-minute break. Because we're running late, during your break, would you please sit together and list your thoughts about group power versus the power you have over the group and any thoughts you have on rejection/exclusion. Choose a spokesperson if that makes it easier.

Back here by ten past guys. We'll check out Nature Vs Nurture too."

GROUP POWER VS INDIVIDUAL POWER

Coach: "Welcome back. Did you have fun putting your thoughts together? Did you choose a spokesperson?"

Max: "Yes. I'm the spokesperson, Coach. We got into the subject during our break, didn't we guys? First, now we understand what we're up against, we're not so worried about being rejected or excluded. We agreed that for young people who have no understanding of our survival programming, it would be super intimidating. Separating from the tribal family and not being accepted by our peer group, feeling like we have no support, is dangerous and scary territory for a young person.

Our thoughts about 'the group':

- We all agreed, we'd be super upset if we were rejected or excluded.

- Now we understand the survival programs, when the group gangs up wanting us to conform, we'd be cool, we'd shrug and say: *"That's just the group behaving as it was programmed to behave."*

- The group needs to control us, or it will lose its power.

- The group wants us to behave 'like sheep' following the leader.

- Conforming with the group leads to mediocrity.

- The group cares jack about the individual; it's all about itself.

- Fear of rejection or exclusion intimidates most of us to stay huddled in group acceptance. People of all ages are scared to liberate themselves from the group, whether its family, generational or any group they belong to and the status quo.

Our power over the group:

- The system conditioned us to think we can't be different, but we think 'different' is okay now that we understand survival and group power.

- We all know the group can be cruel and heartless when it wants us to conform or goes after someone because they're 'different'.

- Now we understand the group's place in our survival, we see it as the group using the threat of rejection or exclusion as a way of forcing and controlling us... you know: *"Conform or we'll boot you out!"*

- It's in our best interests to always have the courage to walk away.

We came up with a few thoughts on rejection with Bethy's help Coach:

- People who made their mark in history, like the impressionist painters, Claude Monet and Auguste Renoir and great architects like Frank Lloyd Wright Snr. had to break away from group conformity and mediocrity to express themselves as individuals. Like Steve Jobs too.

- Those non-conformists were slammed and rejected as being 'black sheep', but they're the ones who go down in history as the great influencers, leaders, and martyrs of their time.

- We decided we'd rather be branded 'black sheep' than follow the leader if we feel strongly about something. We align with *Jonathan Livingstone Seagull.*

That's it, Coach."

Coach: "Wow! You've excelled Heroes! Such a great grasp on group power Vs individual power. I'm blown away!

Okay, now let's quickly cover the final topic for today."

NATURE VS. NURTURE

Coach: "The subject we are about to investigate may appear a little left field, but hey *'Making Friends with Yourself'* is anything but conventional, so let's add more left field stuff, shall we? ☺

We've talked a lot about our automatic subconscious reactions in the last couple of days, haven't we? Now let's trial it. I'll mention one word and I want you to give me your instant reaction, no thinking. Go around the winners' circle starting with Grace this time...

What's your immediate reaction to the word Astrology. Go...

Grace: "Interesting."

Tim: "Questionable."

Queenie: "Enlightening."

Max: "Is BS one word?"

Bethy: "Believable."

Coach: "Wow! First, we'll accept BS is one word Max. Interesting! The boys find the subject doubtful, the girls think it's reasonable and possible. How do you feel about your instant reaction, without thinking? Amazing, isn't it? Your judgement on one subject is already formed! No thinking... game over. Imagine how many judgements you have formed without your awareness!**

Most of us know our Sun sign, don't we? The reason Astrology is included in this course is to draw your attention to your Moon sign and its position in your Natal chart. Your Natal Chart contains the positions of all the planets etc. the moment you were born.

The only information you will need to access this information is the date, time and place of your birth. Google, your local bookshop or a professional astrologer can help locate your Moon sign.

Knowing your Moon sign will beam valuable light on your inner child and its natural emotional state, without the effects of nurturing. Working with your core nature and knowing how you tick is a wonderful gift. It could also give you direction in a career path that is aligned with your nature.

Gentlemen, are you willing to override your negative reactions and check your Moon signs?"

Tim and Max together: "Yes. We'll check them out Coach."

Coach: "Ladies, please do the same. That will be your homework. Does anyone know their Moon sign?"

Bethy: "Yes. I have a Scorpio moon. It's been helpful. I don't fight my nature. Some of its suggestions are detective, psychologist and surgeon; excelling in careers that involve research, transformation and deep investigation. I think anything to do with research appeals to me and it fits in with my need for solitary time. It's coming together, but I haven't decided on my career yet."

Coach: "Bethy is ahead of us guys.

Something fascinating for me, over the years each group I coach seems to fall into certain career categories, like professional, trades, hospitality, etc. Let's find out what your bias is tomorrow when we review your Moon signs. Write your discoveries in Heroes' Notes.

We'll be investigating your age group tomorrow: are young people rebelling or is there more to it? Enjoy the rest of your day. See you here at 8.30 am sharp."

HEROES' NOTES

HOMEWORK: NATURE VS. NURTURE

What is your Moon sign? Has it helped you understand yourself on a deeper emotional level? How?

....

....

....

....

....

....

....

....

....

....

....

What broad career choices does it suggest?

....

....

....

DAY 3:

STAGE 2 – REBELLION OR SOMETHING MORE?

REVISION AND INTRODUCTION

Coach: "Good morning, everyone. Ready for another big day?"

Heroes: "Yes, Coach!"

Coach: "Okay. Did everyone discover their Moon sign? Revelations... anyone?"

Tim: "I was wrong about Astrology, Coach. I have a Pisces Moon which has a supporting nature. I could never understand why I had such a basic need to help and support people. Even my basketball coaching is supportive. There were heaps of other things I found interesting too. But that's the one that makes so much sense to me. I'll investigate the supporting professions in sport like Personal Trainers, Physiotherapists and Sports Psychologists. I can set up my own business, supporting lots of people and recruit other professions to work with me as a kind of 'one stop' sporting clinic. It's given me all kinds of inspired ideas. I know my parents have other plans for my profession. It'll be a gutsy move, as Max says, but I'll have to summon the courage to talk to them about my career choices. I agree with Queenie... *'life shouldn't be this hard!'* Thanks Coach."

Coach: "Great story, Tim. I can see your Moon sign has inspired you. Interesting, isn't it? Grace? Any revelations for you?"

Grace: "I discovered my Moon sign is in Aries. Drive, ambition and leadership. Professions that involve some risk-taking and innovation where I can take charge and head up projects. My career choice can't be boring, or I'll lose interest. Careers mentioned included entrepreneur, military and motivational speaker. I started public speaking classes last year and adding motivation to the speeches really inspires me. I'll investigate what communication courses are available and see where that leads."

Coach: "Wow Grace! How about you Queenie? Did you check out your Moon sign?"

Queenie: "Yes, Coach. I have a Taurus Moon. This is an earth sign which means stability, practicality and perseverance. Taurus Moon people appreciate beauty, and they like the opportunity to build something. They also like financial stability. I love the idea of working for myself. The career I'm attracted to is interior design. It fits in with my love of beautiful things, drawing and colour and a perfect fit working with people but also time on my own to develop concepts for my clients. I see that career as a win-win."

Coach: "Another wow, Queenie. I'm loving this! We're off to a great start today, Heroes! How about you Max? Did you overcome your negative reaction to Astrology and find out your Moon sign?"

Max: "Yes, I thought astrology was BS! It was a kneejerk reaction! Coach was right! We are on rote! **I'll never forget my kneejerk reaction to Astrology. It will serve as a valuable life lesson.** Thanks Coach.

I have a Libran Moon. That means balance and harmony. We like to resolve conflicts, work in collaborative environments bringing people together and fostering positive relationships. We're natural mediators. My career choices need to balance my independence and my social needs. Career ideas were Justice/The Law, public relations, psychotherapy, counselling, teaching. Plenty to think about Coach."

Coach: "It's my turn to tell you, Heroes, how amazing I think you all are. I love advances! You've excelled well past my expectations! I can see this group is likely to go down the professional careers path. So interesting."

Bethy: "Coach, with respect, what's your Moon sign?"

Coach: "Bethy, I'd like to save divulging my Moon sign till Day 5 when I can add more information and another angle for you. Remind me, okay Bethy?"

Bethy: "Okay Coach."

Coach: "Now, (rubbing his hands together) let's get into today's session... very exciting! Day 3 will explain a lot of things including your physical, intellectual and emotional development and what's really going on *now* in your transitioning time zone.

If your authority figures thought ahead, they could relax... knowing most of us turn out okay; in fact, most become 'meek and mild'. Why? Anyone?"

Bethy: "Because they don't know about our programmed need to belong to a group, its conforming 'pack' mentality and fear of rejection."

Coach: "Great answer, Bethy. Anymore?"

Grace: "We've been conditioned to think we all have to be the same."

Coach: "That's right Grace. We've been conditioned to think 'different' is a stigma. There's one more. Anyone?"

Tim: "Fear of upsetting people if we choose something different. I'm thinking of my situation with my parents and standing up to them regarding my career choice."

Coach: "Excellent comparison Tim. Parents are, of course, generally a lot more important than 'others'. But yes, not having the courage to stand up and say what you want or need, no matter who they are.

All the reasons you identified keep us locked into our programming and our conditioning, eventually leading most of us into the 'meek and mild' category.

As discussed yesterday, your childhood model's survival beliefs, attitudes and copied behaviours automatically continue throughout your life. You discovered that it is possible to update those old beliefs and not react subconsciously. Some examples were Time and change, Choices, the Childhood image and of course your subconscious reaction to Astrology. All okay with this?"

Heroes: "Yes, Coach."

Coach: "Now, let's find out why your age group is labelled rebellious."

REASONS YOUNG PEOPLE ARE LABELLED REBELLIOUS

Coach: "The words 'teenagers and rebellious' are often linked to your age group, aren't they? Why? Anyone?"

Queenie: "We are separating from our tribal family and forming a new alliance with our peer group/our generation. Separating, challenging and questioning previous generations is seen as rebellious."

Coach: "Yes. Great answer Queenie! Anymore thoughts on why you conflict with your authority figures in this transitional stage?"

Max: "Because we're no longer children and we want some independence. We'll soon be the next generation to run the show."

Coach: "Another great answer. Thanks Max. Anymore?"

Bethy: "Because we need privacy. We're closer to an adult hormonally than we were as children."

Coach: "Another fabulously super-sensitive answer from Bethy, we've come to expect. Any more thoughts?"

Grace: "We want to be heard and taken seriously."

Coach: "Yes. You want to be heard and taken seriously. A great reason, Grace. How about you Tim? Any thoughts?"

Tim: "We are no longer children. We want a say in our lives."

Coach: "Another great answer. Thank you, Tim. I think you have a good grasp on why your generation looks rebellious.

Now let's find out what's going on in your brain."

REWIRING & RESTRUCTURING OF YOUR BRAIN

Coach: "Have you heard of the Dunedin Study?"

Heroes: "No Coach."

Coach: "You're going to love this! The Dunedin Multidisciplinary Health and Development Study, known as 'The Dunedin Study', started in 1972 when The University of Otago Medical School in Dunedin, New Zealand, began the ultimate Nature Vs Nurture test of 1,037 children born in Dunedin between 1st April, 1972 – 31st March, 1973. This study is the longest of its kind and is ongoing and has the support of governments and industry world-wide.

The study discovered, among other things, that between the onset of puberty through to age 25, the intellectual brain is a work in progress being rewired and restructured – beginning with *'physical co-ordination and motor skills'*, then *'emotional reactions'*. *'Judgements and control'* begin about 21 years of age, completing their journey around 25.

The reason your age group has such *intense emotional reactions*, is because there are two systems in your brain's Limbic system that are developing simultaneously. The difference in development time between the two systems can lead to teens making decisions based on emotions rather than logic, experiencing intense mood swings and being more prone to impulsive behaviours.

So, you see my Heroes, there are valid reasons why you experience such intense emotional reactions and mood swings and are prone to impulsive behaviours at your age.

The Dunedin Study also found that teenage offending is the norm rather than the exception. Crime is common among teens; they are looking for excitement, not able to think of consequences. I'd like it on the record, I'm not endorsing behaviour outside the Law, especially criminal behaviour.

Is this making more sense of your lives Heroes?"

Heroes in unison laughing: "We thought it was our hormones making us look unglued, but it's our brain as well! Thanks Coach."

Coach: "My pleasure! Let's find out more about Stage 2 in your development."

STAGE 2 OF YOUR ONGOING DEVELOPMENT

Coach: "Stage 2 is a bid to gain youthful independence over childhood dependence. You are no longer children. You are growing up, preparing to be the next generation to run the show, as Max said. Caught in the time zone of neither child nor adult, young people often struggle to make sense of this transitional stage. How was my summation?"

Heroes in unison: "Good Coach. There's a lot going on."

Coach: "Yes, there sure is. A lot more than meets the eye. Let's discuss what is going on, what's new and what's confronting in your transitional stage. Remember your intellectual brain is rewiring and restructuring itself.

What overall changes have you noticed in this stage? Who'd like to start?"

Max: "Physical changes in our appearance."

Coach: "Yes. Definitely. Instead of me commenting, identify one after the other what has changed or is changing for you. Round the winners' circle."

Bethy: "Seeking a sense of privacy."

Grace: "Trying to separate from childhood."

Tim: "Hormones and changing into a sexual being."

Queenie: "Comparing yourself to others in your peer group, not always favourably."

Max: "Noticing the opposite sex and admiring a few of your own sex."

Bethy: "Trying to decide on a career path or a course."

Grace: "Trying to keep up with all the expectations placed on us all at once."

Tim: "Feeling pressure in different ways from parents, teachers, and other authority figures and thrown into the self-responsibility thing."

Queenie: "Feeling awkward or a bit clumsy. I'm not sure anyone else is feeling this."

Bethy and Max in unison: "Yes! Me too!"

Tim: "Seeking to express yourself somehow, not so much in words, but um, it's like emotional expression. Like I do with basketball. Is anyone else doing this?"

Max: "Wow... that's well explained, Tim. I know emotional expression relieves a lot of my tension. Like when I play a musical instrument and get swept up in its vibrations."

Grace: "Interesting. What musical instrument does that for you Max?"

Max: "My heavy metal bass guitar. Most people think it's a base guitar, but it's a bass guitar. It has four strings not five as in a regular guitar. Bassist players play simpler lines and chords... more the melodies that sync with the drummer as the rhythm section. Anyway, that's my way of expressing myself with or without words."

Tim: "Wow! You really are my Hero, Max."

Bethy: "I've just thought of one more change. I identify betrayal or disloyalty as a major change. Like someone posting or texting your secrets or private pics. Maybe disloyalty has always been there, but I'm becoming more aware of it now, especially with social media. Does anyone else identify with this?"

Heroes in unison: "Yes… me too!"

Coach: "I'm impressed. You've just covered everything on my list, now I'll add betrayal and disloyalty. Thanks Bethy. We hear a lot about betrayal between friends, betrayal in love, and betrayal in social media, don't we?

Tim brought up the subject of expressing himself. Emotional expression is an important part of expressing ourselves, releasing tension, not always using words. More on emotional expression and its importance in our lives tomorrow.

Now, let's find out where your pressures are coming from."

WHERE ARE YOUR PRESSURES COMING FROM?

Coach: "Do you feel pressure from:

- Your family – may be your tribal or extended family?

- Your teachers?

- Maybe pressure to conform with your peer groups?

- Yourself – putting pressure on yourself with questions like, "Will I ever be enough? Will I ever be as good as them?"

- Other pressures you may be feeling like the changeover to self-responsibility.

Remember: you are operating through your childhood model where you had no responsibility for yourself. Do you think your childhood model is a help or a hindrance?"

Tim: "I think it's a hindrance, especially when we don't know it exists. The beliefs, attitudes and behaviours in the Childhood Model locks us into unconscious positions and our inner child's comfort zone boundaries, like my example of transitioning into self-responsibility."

Queenie: "Yes. Self-responsibility can add a lot of pressure. Not responsible for anything as a child to being responsible for everything, with no lead-up time to get used to the idea. Suddenly it's an expectation."

Coach: "Excellent summation Tim and Queenie. Do you all agree?"

Grace and Bethy: "Yes, Coach."

Max: "Self-responsibility was drummed into me by my mum and dad and my two older sisters. I like the power I feel from self-responsibility, but I feel other pressures."

Coach: "Okay. Except for Max, we all agree transitioning into self-responsibility can create pressure. What about pressures from your family, teachers, your peer group, and your very critical, judgemental self? I'd like each of you to nominate the area or areas you are feeling pressure from. Let's go around the winners' circle starting with Max this time."

Max: "I feel pressure to join in with my peer group, Coach, and when my teachers see that I pullback from the group thing, they're on my back to join in and socialise more too. I'm lucky, I have support from my parents. We all need support, especially in this transition."

Coach: "Thank you for your honesty, Max. We all need support, especially in a transitional phase. Feeling ostracised from the tribal family and your generation can have devastating consequences, as we know. Your turn Bethy."

Bethy: "Like Max, my pressures come from my teachers reminding me to join in more and my mum worries about me not joining in too. I'm okay being around people but I'm not a joiner… and that's okay with me. I learn a lot by watching people and it helps me write my short stories."

Grace: "I mostly feel pressure from my teachers too. They think I can do better and should be getting higher grades. They have high expectations of me, and they nag me to do more academically."

Tim: "I feel constant pressure from my parents. They ride me to keep up my A grades. They have huge plans for me… to be the first doctor or lawyer in our family."

Queenie: "I criticise myself a lot. I'm very judgemental of myself and I worry that I'm not as good as others in my peer group. Although it's not mentioned, I think we're highly competitive, and of course, there's always that fear of rejection/exclusion. I think that's what keeps us 'tight'."

Coach: "Thank you, my Heroes. That's one of the best explanations of teen pressures I've heard in my courses. Congratulations! As I've said before... I love your honesty. I would like to ask Grace a little more about her pressures. Grace, why do think your teachers expect more from you?"

Grace: "I love my dancing classes and the competitions we win, but I feel very pressured by some of my teachers to choose a career path. Maybe they think I'm wasting my academic potential."

Coach: "That would be exactly what your teachers are thinking, Grace. You have time on your side, and the ability to do both if you wish. Your dancing is your emotional expression, and your intellectual capabilities will shine through, no doubt, when you choose your career path. Your Aries Moon will help you figure that out.

Queenie, I'd like to ask you why you think you are not as good as others in your peer group. You mentioned it yesterday too."

Queenie: "I'm not popular like some in my peer group Coach. I compare myself with them. I'm quiet and I'm not social... even the things I like to do are solitary. I feel I'm on the outside looking in sometimes. Your explanation of 'the force' we feel to belong to a group makes a lot of sense to me Coach. Although I don't go along with them all the time, I'm now see belonging as a choice rather than a 'done deal' where I *must* belong.

Also, your explanation on how and why we are all different… that we can never be the same, made immediate sense to me too. Thanks Coach. I've promised to lighten up on myself, remember that I can never be like anyone else and they can't be like me either, and it's okay to be me."

Coach: "Excellent progress Queenie. Congratulations! Did learning about your programmed need to belong to the group and our differences make an impact on anyone else?"

Max: "Yes. It helped me understand why I feel pressure to socialise more. I'm like Queenie, you know, I'm okay not joining in all the time. **I don't want 'the group' running my life.** Your explanation that we are all 'different', helped me to understand and accept that my need for some independence over social pressures, is okay. That it's okay to be me. Thanks Coach."

Coach: "It's great to know where your everyday pressures are coming from especially those pressures related to our survival programming. With new insights you can make sense of them and handle them even better. Your choices at work my Heroes. Anything I've missed?"

Bethy: "I need a lot more sleep in this stage."

Coach: "As usual, Bethy's sensitivity speaks loudly, doesn't it? Does anyone else need more sleep?"

Queenie: "Yes. I do. Even my Mum comments on the amount of sleep I need. She worries that maybe I stay in bed to avoid what's happening in my life and all the changes, but honestly, I'm doing okay, I just need more sleep to help me cope."

Max: "I need more sleep too. If I'm not playing in my band, I take a nap on weekends and I go to bed early most Sunday nights. Like I need more sleep to help me cope with another big week coming up."

Grace and Tim: "We need more sleep too."

Coach: "Well that settles it! Let me assure each of you and your Mum too Queenie, there's perfectly logical reasons why your age needs more sleep. We named them earlier... hormonal changes, physical development, your intellectual brain rewiring and restructuring itself etc. You do need more sleep to help you cope with all the physical, intellectual and emotional changes going on in your transitioning time zone.

Okay it's time to find out why your behaviours are misinterpreted."

WHY YOUR BEHAVIOURS ARE MISINTERPRETED

Coach: "The more I understand your time zone Heroes, the more I'm convinced it's *not* rebellion! Anyone with any thoughts or feelings on this?"

Queenie: "Generally, teens are not trying to upset anyone, but our change in appearance and behaviour, questioning and sometimes conflicting with previous generations, makes us *appear* rebellious. Surface stuff, Coach."

Coach: "Excellent evaluation Queenie. Surface stuff! Love it! Any other thoughts or feelings?"

Tim: "We can't stay children forever. This is our first step towards creating a new identity aligned with the adult we are becoming. We need to step away from our tribal family at some stage. Oh! I must remember that when I bolster my courage and speak to my parents about my career choice! Wow! **Another light bulb moment! Three now.** Thanks Coach."

Coach: "Well done Tim. Any questions? No? Okay, let's check more variables to give you a much bigger picture of the conflicts confronting you in your time zone.

We know your physical appearance has changed significantly... years ahead of your emotional and intellectual development. You are taller and taking on an adult's shape. Because you are now closer in physical size to an adult, your parents and authority figures often consider that you can think like an adult too. We know that's not possible. Why? Anyone?"

Bethy: "Our intellectual brain is being rewired and restructured and won't be fully developed until we are about 25 years old."

Coach: "Yes. Thank you, Bethy. All okay with this?"

Heroes in unison: "Yes, Coach."

Coach: "Let's add some balance to all the conflict going on in your life:

Remember, your parent or parents may still be thinking of you as their 'baby', the little kid who tried to please their mum and dad. Now your parent/s are confronted with a stranger living under their roof, questioning their rules, having opinions and wanting more freedom. Does this add balance?"

Heroes: "Oh! We've only seen our position through our eyes!"

Coach: "It's okay… most of us only see our position through our eyes. If your carers have not considered your hormonal changes and your obvious need for more privacy, it may seem like they are stepping into your space. I know from previous course members and Bethy mentioned it too; privacy is important for teens and young people. A big change from being a child.

It may also seem like your carers' and your authority figures' demands on you are totally excessive; expecting you to keep your room tidy, get good results, be respectful and responsible, care for your appearance, don't be late for class, clean up after yourself, get out of bed, brush your teeth, do your hair, stop talking on the phone, turn the noise down, get off your PC. Have I missed any?"

Heroes conversing then laughing: "You forgot, get your assignments in on time!" ☺☺☺☺☺

81

Coach: "Oh yes, the old standard. Okay, but you get the idea, right? It seems like your life is a battleground with someone or something bossing you around from morning till night.

And a further complication in your transitioning zone that hasn't been mentioned previously… you are usually financially dependent which can make matters more delicate.

And it's not just on the home front and your teachers; your peers criticise and make fun of you, even if you appear slightly different to them, not to mention your self-criticism.

Queenie gave us her excellent example of self-criticism and self-judgement, didn't she? But there is another perfectly valid reason why you may be feeling different. Want to guess? Anyone? No? It's your ego!

Have you heard of the 1970's song, "Ego is not a dirty word"? – sung by the late Graeme 'Shirley' Strahan (1952-2001)."

Max: "It was a Skyhooks song. They were a popular Australian rock band."

Coach: "That's right. Thanks Max. Just so you know, your ego and your intellectual brain are keyed into 'exterior'. Your ego is concerned with its exterior image; your intellectual brain gets its information from exterior sources. Your ego likes to think of itself as separate, even superior to others. It wants you to think of yourself as an individual… to be the best you, you can be.

The ego is a balancing act and a blend between its demands on you to feel superior to others and your awareness of others and the world around you. Great leadership qualities, Heroes, when you get the balance right.

Okay, let's take our 30-minute break now. See you back here at quarter to when you'll confront your seducers. Another big hour coming up Heroes!"

KNOW YOUR SEDUCERS

Coach: "A change of pace now, Heroes. In your journal you'll find a set of questions under the heading, 'Know your seducers'. They are included in this course to make you even smarter and a whole lot wiser.

Let's work with the Universe. You were born self-protective with your feelings, senses, intuition and fear all keeping you safe. Now let's add some up-to-date information to add to your self-protective arsenal.

According to my previous students, 'Know your seducers' and 'Liberating your groundless beliefs' have become two of the most self-empowering but also confronting topics in this Course. We'll find out what you think tomorrow.

These subjects dig deep and help to broaden your understanding of yourself, adding a lot more self-protection and making you less vulnerable to people who will unconscionably take advantage of your age groups' idealism and naivete... no offence!

Seducers, real or imagined, all have power over you. In this sense, seducers are your soft spots or your blind spots. In other words, what seduces you are not always logical, but rather, connected to your heart, an emotional response. They are personal and therefore won't be discussed.

Knowing what your seducers are, can make the difference between wisdom, vulnerability and getting ripped off in the outside world. There are no right or wrong answers. Your answers speak to you from your heart. Be prepared to be surprised.

Okay Heroes, take 15 minutes to silently and privately answer the first set of questions listed in your journal. Then I'll check in with you and find out how you're feeling about the information you are unloading. Like I said, be prepared to be surprised. Let me know if you have any questions."

Apart from your family and friends, is there anything you believe you can't live without? Please list them.

....

....

....

If you find it difficult to be on your own, do you know why?

....

....

....

To feel okay about yourself, do you need to be in the spotlight? Do you need recognition, kudos, compliments, appreciation or notoriety? Do you need to feel smarter or be the most popular? Why?

....

....

....

Now the opposite to the above question, to feel okay about yourself, do you prefer to stay out of the spotlight, to be quiet, to not give an opinion, to not say what you want or need? How does this make you feel? Where does this thinking come from?

....

....

....

Fairytales:

Little girls were inducted into fairy tales and idealism. You loved all the prince and princess stories, didn't you? Movies like 'Pride and Prejudice' and 'Pretty Woman' still have grown-up ladies swooning. Perfectly okay if you are aware...

Are you seduced by charm? Are you a romantic? Must there always be a happy ending? List anything else that makes you feel vulnerable:

....

....

....

Do you always have to be the nice guy? Why? Did you copy someone?

....

....

....

Do you love the material things in life? Do you have to wear the latest fashion? Set the trend? Any others?

....

....

....

Coach: "How are you going with your lists? Any questions? All okay? Yes? Another few minutes' guys."

Naivety:

Are you idealistic? Do you believe everyone, including your friends, have the same ideals as you, that everyone has your principles? Do you believe no-one could be corrupt or hurtful in real life – only in the movies?

....

....

....

A soft heart:

Do you have a soft heart? Do you always feel sorry for someone with a sad story or who is in a tough situation? How does the sad story affect you?

....

....

....

Trust:

Are you a trusting person? Do you take everyone at their word, at face value, like you did as a little kid? Ask yourself: *'What is my trust based upon?'* What would you do if your soft heart and/or your money are being tested? Will you have the courage to say no?

....

....

....

Deserving:

Is there anything you believe you don't deserve. Why? Who said so?

....

....

....

Jealousy:

Is jealousy a seducer of your power? Are you jealous of anyone or anything? What do they have that you think you can't have? Where are those thoughts coming from?

....

....

....

Blaming:

Blaming lets you off the hook. You don't have to be responsible for anything that is happening in your life when you blame. The little kid blames when he thinks he might get into trouble. Blaming separates you from your power. Are you a blamer? When are you likely to blame? Why?

....

....

....

Now the opposite: Do you blame yourself when things go wrong? How is that working out for you? Little kids even blame themselves for divorce! *"I should have been better or not caused so much trouble."* How do you feel when you blame yourself?

....

....

....

Do you avoid?

If yes, what kind of things do you avoid doing or saying? List the benefits.

....

....

....

Victim Mentality:

A victim mentality makes you believe you have no power, that you are helpless, like a child. Do you have a victim mentality? When do you feel like a victim? How do you feel? Do you feel sorry for yourself?

....

....

....

Coach: "Okay, time's up. If you haven't finished naming your Seducers, please be sure to finish your answers tonight."

LIBERATING YOUR GROUNDLESS BELIEFS

Coach: "How are you going Heroes?"

Tim: "I've never come across this kind of information before. It's very confronting but empowering."

Max: "It's packing reality into my life, that's for sure. I'm seeing everything in powerful new light. Thanks, Coach."

Coach: "Good to know gentlemen. How about the ladies? How are you feeling about these subjects?"

Queenie: "It's more personal power. I'm seeing what I'm up against... I'm up against me and my beliefs, not the group in most cases, but my beliefs!"

Grace: "I feel the same as Queenie. I had no idea I was so vulnerable."

Bethy: "It's life changing information for me too. I didn't know I created my own challenges, mostly from idealism and my conditioning."

Coach: "That's great, I'm pleased for everyone. Liberating your groundless beliefs especially at your age will give you a fabulously powerful and deeper understanding of yourself too. Got your pens ready? Okay, 15 minutes then I'll check on how you are going. Any questions, I'm here."

What are your negative beliefs about yourself?

Is it true/are they true? Who said so? Where's the proof, the hard evidence?

....

....

....

Power:

Who or what do you give your power to? For example, do you hand your power over to someone who you think is more attractive, stronger, or smarter than you? Are you dependent on that person in any way?

....

....

....

Who makes you feel powerless? What do they get out of bullying or intimidating you?

....

....

....

On the flipside, what makes you feel empowered?

....

....

....

Self-respect:

How you treat yourself or think of yourself is a learnt behaviour and a belief from childhood. Do you treat yourself with respect? If not, why not?

....

....

....

Do you praise yourself for passing an exam or getting a good assignment result? Do you compliment yourself on your appearance? Why not?

....

....

....

Do you appreciate how much effort you have put into yourself to get to where you are today? If not, why not? What can you start with?

....

....

....

Your uniqueness:

How are you different? What makes you unique from others in your peer group?

....

....

....

Do you appreciate and accept your differences? How? If not, why not?

....

....

....

Coach: "How's everyone going?"

Heroes: "Okay Coach."

Coach: "Keep going with your answers. I'm here, if you have any questions."

Relationships:

It's a fact that relationships change! It's not personal – it's the way life works. We all move forward on different frequencies and in different directions. Do you still have the same friends you had eight or ten years ago? Have any relationships changed for you? Do you miss any of them? Have you left a relationship that was not working for you? Did you leave old relationships behind when you changed courses and met new friends?

....

....

....

(The secret is to enjoy each other's company when you are together and on the same frequency but know this can change and that you will be okay.)

Do you have an abundance or a scarcity mentality? In other words, is your glass half full or half empty? Your way of thinking is making a big difference to what you are attracting into your life. Half full or half empty... where does your thinking come from?

....

....

....

Secrets:

Early in personal relationships, you may be tempted, even eager, to divulge your secrets or some of your secrets to impress. Be careful, remember loyalties can change. Are there any secrets you wished you'd kept to yourself? Why?

....

....

....

Coach: "Okay Heroes, it's approaching midday. Again, completing any unfinished answers will be your homework. Your answers contain immeasurable amounts of powerful, self-protective wisdom. Remember, no right or wrong answers... just getting to know yourself on a deeper level. Enjoy unravelling more mysteries about yourself tonight.

See you back here at 8.30 am sharp for Day 4. Tomorrow's subject will be 'The power of your emotional life'. Have a great afternoon, Heroes."

HEROES' NOTES

....

....

....

....

....

....

....

....

....

....

....

....

....

....

....

....

....

....

DAY 4:

THE POWER OF YOUR EMOTIONAL LIFE

REVISION AND INTRODUCTION

Coach: "Good morning, Heroes. How's everyone this morning? Did you finish your homework? You're very quiet this morning. What's going on?"

Grace: "I think I speak on behalf of everyone when I say we're all feeling a bit overwhelmed, Coach. We love the questions and our deeper understanding of ourselves, but I guess we weren't expecting it to be so confronting."

Coach: "Oh! I get that! Thank you, Grace. Yes, it is confronting. I remind you… this is an anti-suicide course for young people. If I tippy toed around these subjects, or worse, not mentioned them at all, would you be smarter and wiser? This course is about self-preservation. I'm taking sides with the Universe and giving you more self-protective armour to work with when you're 'out there' and if things get tough. Do you understand why these questions should be part of this course?"

Heroes: "Yes, Coach."

Coach: "Was there anything that particularly concerned any of you or was it all the questions on mass, that *felt* overwhelming?"

Heroes: "All the questions all at once."

Coach: "I agree. I've had this conversation with previous Course Heroes many times who felt the same. I'll add here, there is another reason you may be feeling overwhelmed. We'll touch on that a little later this morning.

In the meantime, let's turn your overwhelm into something positive. Think of your answers as a self-protective shield, not only for this stage in your life, but for your future. Can you reinterpret this information in a more constructive light. Anyone?"

Max: "I was looking at how vulnerable I am without this knowledge. It was scary Coach! Did it scare anyone else?"

Tim: "Yes. It's scary to see how vulnerable we are, without knowing it!"

Max: "I realised too, how much baggage I'm carrying around about me that's not true, stuff that needs liberating. I'm going to change my 'scary' interpretation and see my seducers and groundless beliefs as my kryptonite. I'll use it in my next set of lyrics. Thanks Coach."

Tim: "Great idea Max. I'll see my answers as my kryptonite too."

Coach: "Wow! Kryptonite! Max, what a fabulous way of reinterpreting this powerful information. Thank you. Does everyone know what kryptonite is?"

Bethy: "Kryptonite was Superman's weakness depriving him of his powers."

Coach: "Yes. Thanks Bethy. Does everyone now see yesterday's questions reinterpreted as your kryptonite?"

Heroes: "Yes, Coach."

Coach: "Who else would like to voice their feelings?"

Bethy: "Even though it was a bit of a shock, it's given me great insights into myself and my vulnerability. I can also use the word kryptonite in my short stories to help my Heroes on their journeys too. They'll really get it! Thanks Max and thanks Coach."

Queenie: "At first, I felt a bit anxious wondering what might come through. Now I've aired my seducers, and I know what baggage I need to liberate, I feel stronger, like I'm on my side for the first time with all this new, self-protective information. I'll be able to cope better now. Thanks Coach."

Coach: "Thank you Bethy and Queenie. You both have great, new coping stories. Even better, you won't forget this positive life experience. Grace. How are you feeling now?"

Grace: "I'm now seeing this information as more inner strength, to help keep me safer. I hadn't thought of it as exposing my kryptonite. I just saw it as overwhelming. Sorry Coach."

Coach: "No need for apologies Grace. Everyone... understand this Course is for Heroes and your self-preservation. Confronting ourselves head on is heroic. I don't call you 'my Heroes' without good reasons. Please speak to me privately if there is anything in your answers that concerns you. Okay?"

Heroes in unison: "All good now Coach. Thank you."

Coach: "Okay. (Coach rubbing his hands together.) Another big day!

Today we are going to tackle your emotional life. We'll focus on its importance, how to access your feelings and the responsibility you have for caring for yourself on an emotional level – a continuing theme throughout your lives.

You've never been taught the value and importance of your emotional life, have you? It should be part of our education and taught as a life skill.

I believe most of our emotional problems begin in childhood when we didn't understand their power or know how to deal with them. When we can't or don't admit to our feelings, they continue replaying themselves. How do your feelings replay themselves? Anyone?"

Bethy: "Our feelings from our subconscious memories react and replay themselves when we're in a similar situation in present time."

Coach: "Brilliant answer! Thank you, Bethy. Everyone got that?"

Heroes in unison: "Yes, Coach."

Coach: "Not convinced guys! We are repeating in present time the same feelings we felt the last time something like this happened. What did I say? Say it like you mean it!"

Heroes shouting: "We are repeating in present time the same feelings we felt the last time something like this happened!"

Coach: "Yes… excellent! Your feelings are the closest and most intimate part of who you are. Your feelings separate you from every other person in the Universe. As a child you were aligned with your feelings and your feelings controlled your behaviour. If you were feeling unloved, for example, you behaved as if you were unlovable. If you were feeling strong and confident, that was how you behaved. Your inner child's feelings had to be strong – they were a big part of your survival. Everyone on board?"

Heroes: "Yes Coach. We get it."

Coach: "Feelings add meaning to your life. They protect you by making you aware of how you are feeling in every situation. They are biased towards you. **They are your personal radar and your**

constant reality checks. They let you know how and what you are feeling and how you are coping with what is happening in your life at that moment. Remember:

The feelings you don't or won't acknowledge rule your life.

It's easier to ignore your feelings, acting like you're okay, pretending you are fine, everything's fine, when underneath your façade you are hurting, or feeling angry or frustrated. When you sit on your feelings, you are not making friends with yourself, you are creating problems for yourself now and down the line. Got that?"

Heroes: "Yes Coach."

Coach: "Did you know when you don't admit to your feelings, they gather strength in numbers and eventually unbalance your sense of wellbeing. You lose contact with yourself, widening the gap between making friends with yourself and shifting your power up a few notches. Tuning into your feelings is a big part of your new power.

Here's a quote from Richard J. Machowicz, 'Mack', an ex-Navy seal, from his fabulous book, *"Unleash the Warrior Within"* published in 2011.

"The fact that we can change our feelings
means we have power over them. "

Another great read Heroes. Amazing what Navy Seals go through with courage, gutsy determination and tenacity! All okay with this?"

Heroes in unison: "Yes, Coach! We can change our feelings; we have power over them."

Coach: "Said like Heroes! Okay, let's find out how important your feelings really are."

THE SILENT POWER OF YOUR FEELINGS

Coach: "First, you are not your feelings. Feelings create the emotion you are feeling. Feelings are fleeting – whatever the feeling is, it's only there in that precise moment to help you cope with your current situation. Your feelings like you to admit to how you are feeling, positive and negative.

Your feelings are your constant companions – guiding, alerting and intuiting you – making you aware of your connection with yourself, others, the outside world and your position within those spheres.

Acknowledging your feelings is important for:

- Your physical and mental health

- Your emotional wellbeing

- Your motivation and

- Your energy levels.

Working with your feelings is a major shift in your power. Take special note of how you are feeling and what is happening with your solar plexus. Has anyone heard of the solar plexus?

Max: "Yes. It's just below your chest. I feel it a lot from the vibrations when playing in my band."

Coach: "Yes, that makes sense Max. The solar plexus is connected to your central nervous system. Deep, loud heavy metal music and their vibrations would hype up your solar plexus. It's the third chakra in your energy system. If you're interested, you can find out more about your chakras on Google, bookshops etc.

Okay, let's discover how powerful your feelings really are. They can energise you, making you feel strong and fully alert, or the opposite, tired, uninspired and depressed. Let's find out how to access your feelings."

ACCESSING YOUR FEELINGS

Coach: "Recognising and acknowledging your current emotional state is key. It's one of the best kept secrets to an empowered life. Questioning puts you in charge. When you ask yourself regularly:

"What am I feeling?"

You are becoming aware of how you are coping with your current situation. Think of your feelings as a tool Heroes, making you smarter and wiser. Have you thought about your feelings as a tool?"

Heroes: "No, Coach."

Coach: "Basically, you are tuning in to your emotional intelligence. Think of it as a guessing game. *"What am I feeling?"* Because you are new to this, you may have to ask yourself, *'what am I feeling?'* several times.

When you've guessed the correct feeling, you will soften as you resonate with that feeling, effectively neutralising it. Acknowledgement is all your feelings want from you. They belong to the social realm of your life; they like to be acknowledged for all the work they do for you, the same as you like to be acknowledged for all the work you do. Acknowledging your feelings is the Master key to unlocking your courage too. I'm doing all the talking. Any questions, Heroes?"

Queenie: "Are you saying it's our emotional life, not our intellect that connects us to our courage?"

Coach: "Great question Queenie! As you know, we were/are born with our feelings, instincts and senses, all helping us cope 'internally' with what is happening in our daily lives. Around seven years old in recent history, our thinking brain is given priority over our feelings. Yes? The effect doubles when we work with our intellect exclusively, because, as previously mentioned, our ego and intellect connect with our 'external' world.

It is your internal, expanded emotional life that encourages and allows courage to enter your life determining how big your life can be; in this case, courage to push past your childhood fear-based comfort zones. Who'd like to paraphrase?"

Max: "I'll have a go. Emotional expansion determines how big our lives can be. It gives us courage to push past childhood fear-based comfort zones. If we work exclusively with our intellect and ignore our feelings, we bring on the imbalances."

Coach: "Excellent explanation Max. If we work exclusively with our intellect and ignore our feelings, we bring on the imbalances. I'm loving this! Everyone on board?"

Heroes: "Yes Coach. All good."

Coach: "Okay. But we need to know what we are feeling to help us cope even more. I'd like to zoom in on specific incidences, such as when you're feeling:

• sudden, unexpected fearful reactions

• anxious, uneasy or stressed reactions

• overwhelmed.

You now know that most of your fast, fear-based reactions are coming through your childhood subconscious kneejerk reactions. To help you figure out where your fearful reactions are likely coming from, ask yourself:

- Am I moving into unfamiliar and challenging territory?

- Is the little kid in me *not* wanting to leave its comfort zone?

- Is my inner child feeling it won't be able to cope, or it may embarrass itself, because I want to try something new?

- Is my inner child feeling, "*I can't do this!*" or "*I'm not up to this!*"

Heroes, let me ask you this: could your feelings of overwhelm to all the questions you finished last night also be related to your little kid's fearful, subconscious reaction? What do you think?"

Heroes in unison: "Oh! Yes, of course! All those questions all at once could be the little kid in overwhelm, making us feel overwhelmed too!"

Coach: "Yes. Very likely Heroes. You don't have to know who, or why, or what is creating or contributing to your feelings of overwhelm, just admitting to your feeling of overwhelm or whatever the feeling is at the time is all it wants from you. And you did that! Well done! How do you neutralise your feelings Heroes?"

Heroes in unison: "We admit to how we are feeling to neutralise them. Got it, Coach."

Coach: "Any further questions? No? Let's briefly get into 'sledging' to form a powerful, different point of view."

SOCIAL MEDIA 'SLEDGING'

Coach: "Does anyone know what the term 'sledging' means?"

Tim: "Yes, 'sledging' is a slang term used in cricket to intimidate opposing players."

Coach: "Great answer Tim. 'Sledging' is a cricket term that means to bully opposing team players with insulting words and behaviours.

Unfortunately, social media 'sledging' is part of life today. It's cruel, it's shameful, and slagging of others, often written by gutless power-hungry keyboard warriors, who are not willing to show their faces or use their real names, can often be the cause.

If they're picking on you, know that it's not all about you, it's about them wanting recognition, reactions and a social media following; they love the limelight. They want you to bow to their pressure.

Ganging-up against a fellow peer is cowardly. I repeat, your peer group can be one of the cruellest groups in your life. Remember: no-one has to put up with that kind of behaviour. You deserve; we all deserve better. What do Heroes do?"

Heroes: "Heroes have the courage to walk away."

Coach: "Yes indeed. Your power comes from walking away. Think of sledgers as cowards. I know it's not easy but *not* reacting turns the table and has them feeling and looking powerless and cowardly. And remember, popularity is mercurial; it can change very quickly.

If you are or if you have been sledged or ridiculed on social media or in the school grounds or within your peer group, what do you do with your emotional pain?

Admitting to yourself how you are feeling, then talking to someone about your painful feelings is super-hero stuff! Heroes don't hold back! They know when they need help, and they follow through! Do you remember who you chose as your confidant, Heroes?"

Heroes in unison: "Yes Coach."

Coach: "Never forget: your feelings love to be acknowledged. Your emotional life is your courage and your power in many ways. My advice, stay away from social media 'til you feel you can handle any downside.

Now let's briefly look at ways people try to numb their emotional pain."

ADMITTING TO YOUR EMOTIONAL PAIN

Coach: "What are some of the main ways people of all ages try to numb or block their emotional pain? Anyone want to have a go at this?"

Max: "Drugs."

Coach: "Yes Max. Thank you. Drugs, both recreational and prescription. Anyone else?"

Bethy: "Comfort eating."

Tim: "Alcohol abuse."

Coach: "Yes, they are the big ones, aren't they? Your feelings, especially the intense feelings of emotional pain, want you to recognise and admit to them, otherwise, eventually, with so many of your feelings ignored, they will get your attention in far more serious ways. The feelings you don't acknowledge can unbalance your sense of wellbeing too. Got that?"

Max: "I think we realised that the kids who get into drugs, abusing alcohol or food is a way of relieving their emotional pain, *but I didn't connect acting out with not admitting to all their emotional pain.* That really makes sense to me Coach. How about everyone else?"

Heroes: "Yes. It does make sense. Thanks Coach."

Coach: "Admitting to how you feel, even if you have to acknowledge your feelings several times, puts you in the driver's seat. Congratulations Heroes. Smarter and wiser... again!"

Okay. Time for our 30-minute break. It's been heavy going again this morning, hasn't it? See you back here at quarter past. We'll shine a powerful new light on anger. You'll love this!"

A POWERFUL NEW LIGHT ON ANGER

Coach: "Ready Heroes? Get settled. Okay, time to shine a new and powerful light on anger. Most people shy away from the subject, don't they? It's almost taboo! I want my Heroes to understand anger, why it's present in your life and what you can do about it.

First, it's important to understand, anger is on your side. That's right! Anger cares about you; anger wants the best for you. Its presence lets you know you are reaching your limits!

All okay with this? Any comments?"

Tim: "Wow! You are turning this subject upside-down Coach! Anger scares most people. Now you're saying it cares for us and wants the best for us?"

Coach: "That's exactly what I'm saying, Tim. Anyone else with a view?"

Bethy: "My mum tells me to move away from angry scenes and don't get involved."

Coach: "That's good advice Bethy. Your mum is right. But I'm talking about your personal anger, not an angry crowd. Can you see the difference? Any more views?"

Max: "I've seen some pretty ugly scenes out there. But coach is right, I wasn't part of the anger, I was witnessing a crowd's anger. Scary stuff guys. I don't associate it with my personal anger."

Coach: "Thanks Max. Do you all see the difference between a crowd's anger and personal anger? Any other comments? Grace? Queenie? No?

What is anger?

Feelings of anger are stirred when you instinctively feel that you are being ignored or not taken seriously, you've been treated unfairly, or generally disrespected. Anger could also be attached to a regret or missing out on being selected for a promotion or a place in a team sport, for example.

Anger also gets upset with controlling and vindictive behaviour. How often have we heard of a murder when one party retaliated against the controlling behaviour of another? We've all heard of such incidences, haven't we?

How does anger act out when it's ignored?

Anger is an energy that needs plenty of space. It needs to blow off steam. It doesn't like to be ignored or couped-up. Anger becomes furious when you don't or won't admit to its presence – pretending you are okay... everything is okay. You are effectively rejecting its wisdom! Anger is a force, it means business and it's deadly serious.

Heroes, I want you to be aware that when you don't admit to ever *feeling* angry, the feeling builds up to a time when it won't take much to push you over the edge, then it becomes unmanageable, and we see anger erupt. Got that?"

Grace: "So if we ignore our personal anger every time we feel it, eventually we won't be able to control it. Is that what you're saying Coach?"

Coach: "Yes, exactly. Thank you, Grace. When you constantly ignore your anger, eventually, it will become unmanageable. All okay with this?"

Heroes: "Yes, Coach."

Coach: "Let's find out more:

What does anger want from you?

Anger wants your acknowledgement; it wants you to admit to feeling angry; it wants your attention. It works hard for you. It wants you to recognise how important its contribution is to your wellbeing and your life. Its presence indicates your boundaries are being pushed to your limit.

Anger wants the best for you. It's sick and tired of making excuses for some people's behaviours or any unfair expectations they have placed on you. Anger wants you to feel respected and it wants you to acknowledge its presence and respect its position too.

How does this explanation sit with my Heroes?"

Bethy: "Your explanation makes so much sense, Coach. It's like fear is our physical bodyguard and anger is our emotional bodyguard."

Coach: "Wow! Bethy. I've never thought of anger as our emotional bodyguard. Fabulous! I'll use that explanation in future courses. Thank you. Everyone on board with this?"

Queenie: "Coach, you're saying, when we *feel* our anger stirring, we are reaching our limits. Is that right?"

Coach: "Yes Queenie. When we feel angry, we are reaching our limits.

What do you do with your angry feeling?

As we know, anger can terrify some people, so try to find some private space to fume. It's not hurting anyone at this stage.

Getting physical can be a great way to let off steam. Taking some deep slow abdominal breaths, in, hold for a few seconds, then breathing out, works well too. Sit with the feeling, admit to how angry you are. Acknowledgment acts as a pressure valve. Say, for example, *"I'm so angry! I want more respect! I don't deserve this! It's not fair!"* Vent, vent, vent. Allow your anger to lose some of its high energy and intensity… it's good for you. Anger wants you to be aware that you are close to your limits. You are not a machine!

The more space and acknowledgement you give to your anger, the more you take control and the calmer and better you will feel. It's great to let all your angry feelings out. **Thank your anger for its warnings.** Your anger is devoted to you, or as Bethy says, anger is your emotional bodyguard. Your mission is to cut the power of anger the moment you recognise its presence."

Grace: "Is that all we have to do? Just acknowledge our anger and it will go away? Do we have to do that every time we feel our anger stirring?"

Coach: "I love your questions, Grace. When you say, is that all we have to do… just admit you're angry and it will go away? I agree, it sounds simple, but acknowledgement is a powerful tool and a significant pacifier. You are not ignoring anger and pretending it's not there. You have recognised your anger, acknowledged its presence, and you are giving your anger space to vent. You are acknowledging that your boundaries and your limits have been reached which is why your anger is present. You cool its intensity by admitting to its presence. Sometimes you will have to say, *"I feel my anger!" or "I am angry!"* a few times, before its intensity calms down.

To answer your second question, Grace, yes, we do have to go through this process every time we feel our anger stirring. You don't want your anger becoming unmanageable, do you? That's how it got its threatening, scary reputation. Is that a clearer explanation, Grace?"

Grace: "Yes, thanks Coach. When you think of how scary anger can be, admitting to the feeling didn't seem enough. But now I get that admitting to the feeling, even if we have to acknowledge it several times, is powerful enough to pacify anger! Anger wants us to recognise we are reaching our limits and to recognise all the work it does for us as our emotional bodyguard, as Bethy said. I get it now. Thanks Coach."

Coach: "My pleasure Grace. On a personal note: I wasn't allowed to feel or express my angry feelings at all when I was your age. Anger was not allowed or recognised by my family. People are scared of its power and don't know how to respond or what to do with it, so they ignore it! You now know, it won't be ignored! Smarter and wiser Heroes!

Owning and acknowledging your anger will remove its power over you. Feel proud of yourself – it's heroic stuff and another example of your personal power in action. Anger can also be very motivating when used positively. Any questions?"

Heroes loudly in unison: "All good, thanks Coach."

Coach: "Okay. Now I'd like to introduce you to a surprising way anger can present itself. We've all heard of depression, haven't we?"

Heroes: "Yes Coach."

Coach: "No doubt you all know there are many types of depression, but do you know anger can turn inwards? That's right! Instead of coming across in its usual outward, loud and aggressive form, anger can turn inwards and present as a soft fog, blanketing you in sadness, tiredness and a general loss of interest. Owning this type of anger is heroic too! You could ask yourself, *"Why am I so angry with myself?"* Another reason to seek professional advice Heroes.

What's the #1 affirmation for the *'Making Friends'* course?"

Heroes shouting: "It's good to feel my power and it's great to own my power." ☺☺☺☺☺

Coach: "Sure is… now, let's add some light-heartedness."

EMOTIONAL EXPRESSSION/SATISFACTION

Coach: "We touched on emotional expression yesterday. It seems like a long time ago, doesn't it! ☺ We've covered a lot of subjects, but this one is delightful guys. Today, I'd like to give you a fuller explanation, so you are aware of how important emotional expression is to help satisfy your lives.

I think of emotional expression as keeping your emotional life nourished and satisfied. Sounds like an appetite, doesn't it? I think of emotional expression as your appetite for life. It connects you to your core, to your essence. It fuels your highs, lifts your lows, and the nutrition you are feeding your longevity is priceless. It's an emotional state that takes you to a place where you are 'in the flow' and time simply disappears. It's when you are totally involved and committed to something you love to do.

Emotional expression can be a creative endeavour like painting, or it can be an emotional connection to a vision, a calling, fighting an injustice etc.

We are all naturally creative. As little kids we invented ways to play. In fact, playing and creating are ways we connect to our authentic selves. Everything in your life needs creative attention. Boredom creeps in when you are not creating, when you are not making your life or your special relationships new again with your love, vision and creative energy. Your imagination builds newness, making you feel happy and healing you.

What is your emotional outlet, that is, what do you really love to do? We touched on this yesterday. And what other types of emotional expression can you think of?"

Grace: "Mine are dancing and public speaking."

Coach: "Yes. Thank you, Grace. Anymore?"

Bethy: "Writing my short stories and journalling."

Tim: "Coaching basketball is mine. Any coaching job or playing a sport would be a good way to express yourself emotionally, wouldn't it Coach?"

Coach: "Definitely Tim. Getting physical is a good way to express yourself. Anyone else?"

Max: "Playing my guitar and writing lyrics."

Queenie: "Drawing and colour."

Coach: "Yes! All your ideas tick the emotional expression boxes. I'll add acting, building a beautiful garden, designing, decorating, painting. It can be physical, but not always and it can be with or without words. You get the idea. In other words, it's something that helps you forget the pressures of life for a while, releasing your anxiety levels and keeping you out of your resentment zone.

Does anyone know what a resentment zone is?"

Bethy: "Resentments can include anger like when a person is making unfair demands on us or a regret when we didn't stand up for ourselves. It's also when we feel life is all work and no play; that there is no 'me time'."

Coach: "Brilliant, Bethy. All the above, especially when we don't make 'me time' for ourselves. All on board Heroes?"

Heroes: "Yes Coach. Make sure there is 'me time' in our lives."

Coach: "Count on it! Now, let's find out why your emotional relationship with yourself is important."

BUILDING A STRONG EMOTIONAL RELATIONSHIP WITH YOURSELF

Coach: "A strong, positive emotional relationship with yourself embracing self-acceptance is a building block to your individual power.

The relationship you have with yourself is the most important one of all. Do you know why I've repeated this a couple of times? Anyone?"

Bethy: "Because it sets our standards."

Coach: "Yes. A strong emotional relationship with yourself sets your standards, thanks Bethy. It gives you a great base to build on. Who'd like to add another layer?"

Tim: "It can help expand our comfort zones."

Coach: "Another great answer, Tim. We can decide how far we are willing to expand our fear-based comfort zones. Anyone else?"

Max: "How much we are prepared to knuckle under with the group before we decide to pull back and decide for ourselves."

Coach: "Definitely. Thanks Max. Queenie or Grace, any thoughts?"

Queenie: "I do have a question Coach. Does this strong emotional relationship we are building with ourselves become a behaviour?"

Coach: "Wow! Queenie. I had to step back for a moment and think about your question. Yes. It's like your emotional relationship with yourself is setting a new behavioural standard for what you are willing to do for yourself and what you are willing to put up with from others. You are becoming pro-active on your behalf.

Grace, any questions?"

Grace: "All good Coach."

Coach: "Okay. Fantastic! Sorry Heroes, we're out of time. Your homework tonight is meant to be light-hearted. Choose an idol or a role model. Choose more than one if you like. Think about why you're attracted to this person/s, and what qualities you admire. Also, what's the one thing you can start doing immediately to become more like your idols or your role model/s?

Have a great afternoon. See you here at 8.30 sharp for Day 5 – 'Personal Success' the final day of our Course together."

HEROES' NOTES

HOMEWORK – CHOOSING YOUR ROLE MODEL

Do you have a role model? More than one? Think about who you admire or who you'd like to be. You don't have to know that person. He or she can be a movie star, an athlete, someone who courageously won a battle of some kind, maybe an influencer, a life coach, someone you admire in your community, a family member, a friend etc.:

....

....

....

....

Why are you attracted to that person/s? What qualities do you admire?

....

....

....

....

....

....

What's one thing you could do now to be more like your role model/s?

....
....
....
....
....

How will that help you?

....
....
....

Any other comments:

....
....
....
....
....

DAY 5:

PERSONAL SUCCESS

ROLE MODELS

Coach: "Good morning, Team. Another big day coming up. (Coach rubbing his hands together). Did everyone finish their homework? Anything you'd like to share?"

Bethy: "Yes, I'll share. I admire my mum. She's a single mum and she's overcome a lot of adversity. She works hard to support me and to give us a good life. She's a great role model. I hope to emulate all her qualities."

Coach: "They are all fabulous reasons why you've chosen your mum as your role model, Bethy. Anyone else?"

Tim: "I admire the basketball legend, Michael Jordan. I'm not saying I could be like him, but I admire his game, and his personal qualities. I also admire people who have started from scratch and built business empires. Last night I came across several exceptional role models. I'll study their stories and blend the qualities I most resonate with. Thanks Coach."

Max: "I admire the guys in heavy metal bands that have lasted. I'm thinking Metallica, Black Sabbath, Iron Maiden and Slayer. The music industry is tough; you've got to be tougher to survive. I admire their tenacity and their gutsy determination. It looks easy up there on stage, but that image is far from reality. Robert Trujillo is the bassist in Metallica. He's super cool and known for his kindness. I love watching him being interviewed; he's totally grounded. If I wanted to be a singer, I would choose Pantera's vocalist, Phil Anselmo. You've got to hear his voice to believe it guys!

This Course has me thinking Coach, I'd like to do something with young people. I really get them. Counselling came up as a career option for a Libran Moon. I could be a youth counsellor or a youth worker. I *feel* I could do a lot of good work. How do I become one of your franchisees Coach so I can teach this Course too?"

Coach: "Both great choices Tim and Max! Max, I'll arrange a time when we can meet and talk about how you can become a franchisee. You'll be a great role model for young people. Role models can give you direction, especially at your age, and they can lift your spirits when things get tough. How about Queenie and Grace. Would you like to share your thoughts on your role models?"

Queenie: "I admire people who have made something of their lives too. I was thinking last night about a career in interior design and the icons in the world of interiors like Laura Ashley. I love her timeless, gracious interiors. Everything goes in cycles so I could start a new cycle and bring back those classic interiors, with a modern twist. I also love the interiors of Australian, the late Stuart Rattle (1960-2013). Everyone who knows his work loves the fine details in his unique, classical style. I will research their stories and identify their dual qualities. I'm so inspired. Thanks Coach."

Coach: "Wow! We are inspired too, aren't we guys! Thank you, Queenie. We're on a roll. How about you, Grace?"

Grace: "You know I like public speaking. I'm still not sure about my career choice, but I would like motivational speaking to be part of it. I'm inspired too. Thanks Coach. The reason I held back, not admitting to my role model is because I don't want anyone laughing at me. It's probably an odd choice, but I love watching Arnold's interviews and his motivational speeches. I admire all his achievements in one lifetime too. He's a legend. Arnold Schwarzenegger is my role model!"

Coach: "Wow! Grace, I love his interviews and his motivational speeches, and I admire all his achievements in one lifetime too! He is a Legend! What do you think guys?"

Heroes in unison: "You're our Hero Grace! We love and admire him too!"

Bethy inspired: "Oh! After hearing everyone's role model stories, I realise I'm only halfway through choosing my role model. I love my mum, and she will always be my #1 role model. Once I decide my career path, I'll research autobiographies about personalities in that profession and align with the qualities I admire. I'm sure they'll be very motivational too. Thanks Coach, thanks Grace and thanks everyone. Your stories inspire me to dig deeper."

Coach: "Well done Bethy. Another great start to our session today which happens to be called 'Personal Success'."

Bethy: "You asked me to remind you to tell us your Moon sign Coach."

Coach: "Oh! Yes. Thank you for reminding me, Bethy.

Well, like Tim, I have a Pisces Moon. I belong to the supporting network. The teaching, coaching and counselling work I do, helping and supporting others, gets me up each morning, eager to start the day. If you have an emotional connection with your occupation, you'll never work a day in your life. Have you heard that phrase? That's how you do it! By connecting emotionally with your career. What did I just say Heroes?"

Heroes shouting and laughing: "Connect emotionally with your career."

Coach: "Why?"

Heroes shouting: "You'll never work a day in your life."

Coach: "How about this for a fab quote from Steve Jobs:

"The only way to do great work is to love what you do. If you haven't found it, keep looking. Don't settle. As with all matters of the heart, you'll know when you find it."

Coach: "Okay, let's revise your power bases."

REVISION: SURVIVAL & YOUR POWER BASES

Coach: "Let's review the survival system and its boundaries. I want you to go home never forgetting why adolescents, teenagers and young people are driven to fit in and conform with their peer group. Can you remember the programs we were all born into? Anyone?"

Queenie: "We were born self-protective with our feelings, senses and instincts operating."

Max: "Fear is part of our DNA. Fear acts like our personal bodyguard."

Tim: "Our subconscious mind was our memory before we could think. It's still our memory today in the first seven years."

Bethy: "We live in a two-time zone system."

Grace: "If we don't understand the survival system, we live like robots, repeating our childhood beliefs, attitudes and copied generational behaviours as present time subconscious kneejerk reactions."

Coach: "Excellent detail Heroes. What has changed? Anyone?"

Bethy: "We live a lot longer."

Tim: "Our intellectual brain is operating. We can think."

Queenie: "Some individuals are standing up to the group having all the power. They want to decide whether to belong to the group or not."

Coach: "Yes, yes and yes! Thank you. Any questions? No?

Okay, let's find out more about how the group still wants to control you today."

GROUP POWER AND YOU TODAY

Coach: "Let's get to the core:

An understanding of 'the group' and its place in survival for man and all species gives us an edge over 'The survival system'. The Universe gave survival power to 'The group'.

'The group' kept 'the individual' safe and maintained order with its rules and a conforming 'pack' mentality. Back then, it was *'belong to the group or die!'* Conforming with the group was about survival… nothing more. The individual wasn't a concept back then. Fast forward to the 21ˢᵗ Century, the group still wants all the power. All clear on this?"

Heroes in unison: "Yes, Coach."

Coach:

"To remain empowered, the group must control you… it needs you to conform with its 'pack' mentality.

This applies to all groups, not just your peer group and social media groups, but basketball teams, heavy metal bands, book clubs, dancing groups! All of them! Nothing has changed! Life continues repeating itself from one generation to the next to survive. Basic caveman stuff. Let me hear it!"

Heroes shouting: "Yes, Coach. Got it!"

Coach: "Let's review group power:

- You know about our survival programming, group power, fitting in and conforming with their rules.

- You know the group has a 'knuckle under' or be rejected policy. It gangs-up and uses bullying and intimidation to make you conform.

- The group cares jack about the individual.

- You also know your peer group wants you to be the same as them, to dress like them, think like them, be like them.

- The group wants us to behave like sheep, following the leader.

- Conforming with the group leads to mediocrity.

- You know you must give up your individual power to belong to the group. That's the trade-off; give up something to get something else.

Everyone okay with this?"

Heroes in unison: "Yes, Coach."

Coach: "What about today, Heroes? The group still wants the power today, doesn't it? Let's turn the tables and balance the ledger. **What are your power bases over the group?** Round the winners' circle. Who'd like to start?"

Bethy: "I'll start. We were conditioned to believe we can't be 'different'. With our new understanding, different is okay."

Grace: "Our peer group can be heartless, even cruel when they intimidate us with their bullying style behaviour to make us conform with them. When we give them our power, it makes us vulnerable. Today, we have choices."

Tim: "We know we'll be okay with or without group approval or anyone's approval."

Queenie: "It's okay too if we don't fit in, if we're not liked by everyone and not the same. We need to go with our gut and decide for ourselves; choices have consequences, and it will take courage too."

Max: "Now we understand what the group is all about, we have power over them. As I've said before, *'I don't want the group running my life.'*"

Bethy: "The Universe gave power to the group to help us survive. Today, accepting that we are all unique and different, and feeling okay if we don't fit in and conform, is the 21ˢᵗ Century evolving with the individual's rights and choices."

Coach: "Well said, Bethy and excellent responses Heroes! When or if the group starts its conforming campaign against you, what's the most empowering thing you can do?"

Heroes in unison: "We can walk away!"

Coach: "Yes! You can! You can walk away! It doesn't mean running away which has a cowardly sentiment, rather, walking away is heroic. It's powerful and it's awesome... not just in your young years but walking away should be your automatic powerful life preserving reaction throughout your life. When you feel pressure to conform with anyone or a group, you have the courage to walk away.

The group becomes more powerful than you...
only when you give them your power.

COURAGE... PERSONAL SUCCESS

Giving yourself permission to feel okay... without approval from anyone or any group! is your forever power base.

All on board with this? Yes? Okay, let's discover more layers of support when you need it."

LAYERS OF SUPPORT

Tim: "Fear of rejection is the one that concerns me Coach. I mean, even though I know belonging to a group is a survival force, I like being part of my peer group, and my basketball team. It's fun and uplifting for me, especially when I can support someone."

Coach: "Thanks Tim. Fear of rejection is a big part of everyone's life... fear of rejection or exclusion is intimidating, and it keeps most of us conforming with our peer group. We didn't like to be called out and to feel rejected as little kids, and we still don't like to be called out and to feel rejected now. That's why most of us stay huddled in the group. We want to be protected, and we want to *feel* supported and accepted, don't we? It's been programmed into our subconscious and unconscious driven behaviours.

How you feel about belonging to your peer group is a personal choice. If, like Grace and Tim, you are happy fitting in with the group and it feels right for you, then please stick with your gut feeling. If, you are more like Queenie, Max and especially Bethy, then know you are faced with a choice. No matter which choice you make, choices have consequences, and it takes courage to go your own way. All okay with that?"

Tim: "Yes, Coach. It's a choice. You can choose whether you want to belong and fit in with the group and conform with their rules, or whether you choose to be more independent."

Coach: "Yes. Thank you Tim. It's all about our choices. What if we're like Steve Jobs? What if we simply can't, don't or won't fit in and conform? What then?"

Bethy: "I'm okay not fitting in. I like being around people, but I don't want to fit in and conform with them. That's my choice. I know there are sometimes consequences for my behaviour, but I'm okay with that too. I have support from my mum."

Coach: "Thanks Bethy. That's the lead-in to our next point. Let's talk about support and the layers of support. Bethy has support from her mum. Grace and Tim feel supported by 'the group'. Support gives us a feeling of safety.

Most of us want and need support, don't we? That's okay. I want support too, even at my age! So, what do people do who want support but who don't fit in with their peer group and their family?"

Max: "They could find or establish a common interest group like I did when I formed my band. Maybe they could choose a computer club, a team sport or a book club. That way they still get support, and what they have in common keeps them together."

Coach: "A common interest group. Brilliant Max! Yes, but I remind you, even the common interest group will have rules. How about you Queenie? Who besides your school counsellor gives you support? Anyone?"

Queenie: "I didn't mention her before, but when I need extra support or I just want someone to talk to, I phone my grand mum. She's always had my back. We share secrets; I know I can tell her anything. She's so wise, and she makes me laugh."

Coach: "Wow! Queenie. Yes! Grandparents are another great layer of support. Most of us need someone or something that has our back. Even Steve Jobs, a bit of a loner by all accounts, found support in outsiders.

Support layers for Heroes:

• your parents	your peer groups
• common interest groups	grandparents
• school counsellors	a close friend
• psychologists/counsellors	a coach.

We all agree, Heroes need support. They don't hold back, they ask for help ASAP. Do you remember who you chose as your #1 confidant, if things were getting tough?"

Heroes in unison: "Yes, Coach!"

Coach: "Now I'm going to be the devil's advocate. What if your confidant is not available when you urgently need to talk to someone? What would you do? It's my belts and braces formula. ☺

Here's another layer of support. My Plan B for everyone who lives in Australia, is to contact any of the following 24/7 services without delay:

Headspace 1800 650 890

Lifeline: 13 11 14 or text 0477 131 114

Beyond Blue: 1300 22 4636

Suicide Callback service: 1300 659 467

Kids Helpline: 1800 55 1800

For anyone not living in Australia, you'll find similar organisations in your local area. Look them up on Google. They are waiting for your call. Please don't delay, ring today! It's all about back-up and support when you need it.

Talking to someone... getting your feelings out into the open so you can deal with them and take the pressure off you is brilliant! Everyone okay with this? Yes?

Now let's find out how you would handle your own rejection. This will be interesting."

HOW WOULD YOU HANDLE YOUR REJECTION?

Coach: "I'd like my Heroes to tell me what each of you would do if you were rejected or excluded by a group, any group, or anyone, including your tribal family, an individual, a romantic partner, a VIP in your life. *I need to know you will be safe; that you have a plan.*

Just so you know, your reaction to rejection or exclusion will more than likely be emotionally intense. Remember back in Day 3, I introduced you to the Dunedin Study? Yes? They discovered that two parts of the Limbic system in your brain are developing at different speeds which is why your emotional reactions are so intense at your age; another reason why I think rejection and/or exclusion are best handled by professionals.

Let's start with Grace and Tim who like to belong to the group. Grace, what would you do if the group rejected you?"

Grace: "I'm sure I'd cry a lot. I'd journal how I was feeling too. I think the most difficult thing would be facing those people who rejected me. Groups can be heartless if they think you're 'different' or if you don't conform with them. I've watched them pick on other kids. If I was rejected, I would need someone to talk to ASAP that understood intimidation and bullying. I'd see my School Counsellor."

Coach: "Nice approach. Grace would need to speak to someone ASAP that understood intimidation and bullying. She would choose her school counsellor. Tim, what would you do?"

Tim: "I'd not only *feel* devastated, I would also be super embarrassed and I'm sure I'd feel overwhelmed by my emotional reaction. *"How will I face everyone?"* would be a major concern. They'll all be laughing at me. I would lose face, if that makes sense.

I'd lose confidence in myself, and I'd lose trust in others. I'd get physical and shoot hoops for a while. And then, like Grace, I would need to speak to someone ASAP too. Initially, I would choose my basketball coach. He's had a lot of experience, and he's got a great reputation for helping kids with rejection issues."

Coach: "Tim, I like the 'get physical' part of your reaction. Letting off steam and speaking to someone, are both great reactions. Your feeling of losing face means feeling humiliated. Excellent point Tim. That is exactly what rejection feels like. Rejection is humiliation. All Heroes got that?"

Heroes: "Yes, Coach. Rejection is humiliation."

Coach: "Max, what would you do?"

Max: "I wouldn't like to be rejected either, Coach. I'd be like Tim and do something physical for a while. Then I'd talk to my parents. They are my 'go to' when things get tough and then we'd decide what's next. Like everyone, I've seen enough to know when 'the group' has an agenda. We now know it's to control us with fear of rejection or exclusion. *"Conform or we'll boot you out!"* is a nasty method of making us into sheep, but it's the way 'The survival system' works.

Let's face it, after rejection we're still here; maybe a little scarred for the experience, but we are physically okay. It's the *feeling of rejection*, the humiliation and embarrassment; it's the emotional pain that hurts.

I think at some stage in life, if you're going to make anything of yourself, you have to break away from 'the group' mediocrity thing, otherwise it's just us being scared with fear of rejection running our lives."

Coach: "Awesome Max. Thank you. How would you handle your rejection, Queenie?"

Queenie: "I'd be devastated too and stressed. Max is right! Physically, I'd be okay; the battle would be how to handle the emotional pain of rejection. First, I'd admit to how and what I was feeling, then I'd want to speak to one of my school counsellors, fast, but if she wasn't available, I would phone Headspace. I wouldn't know how to deal with my feelings on my own, so *I'd want to speak to someone ASAP to help me with my feelings before things got worse.*"

Coach: "Another great response. I love '*before things got worse*'. Thanks Queenie. Bethy, how would you handle group rejection?"

Bethy: "I'd probably be more philosophical, Coach. The fact that I don't want to belong to a group is giving me some protection, but I wouldn't like to feel rejected or excluded. It would be humiliating and painful.

To console myself, I would probably hum, "It's my life" by Bon Jovi and align with the 'black sheep' throughout history, like Claude Monet.

I doubt I could handle rejection on my own. I'd speak to my mum first, then go from there. *I wouldn't try to handle my feelings on my own, that's for sure.*"

Coach: "Thank you, Bethy.

**Okay. We all agree, we would speak to someone to get our feelings out into the open, so we can deal with them ASAP *before things got worse.*

And we know rejection by your peer group is painful, but it's not worth taking your life! They're not picking on you! It's not personal! You are not a victim! They treat everyone who is** 'different', and/or who doesn't fit in and conform with them, the same. They have been programmed to keep you huddled in the group for survival reasons. That's it... you know more about their agenda, than they do! Who's the powerful one now?"

Heroes in unison: "Thanks Coach. We love this!"

Coach: "Don't forget affirmation #2. Let me hear it Heroes."

Heroes in unison and loud: *"I will not give up my life for anyone or a group. I have the courage to walk away."*

Coach: "Remember: there is nothing wrong with you! The system is rigged against the individual. The Universe gave survival power to the group. Knowing what you're up against is a shift upwards in your power. I remind you:

"No matter how much trouble you're in or
how 'different', desperate or unsupported you feel,
you will get through this. This is a phase... and you will be okay."

Great work. I mean *really* great work, Heroes."

YOUR CHOICES AND THEIR CONSEQUENCES

Coach: "We're nearly done with 'the group' now. (Rubbing his hands together). Just doing the belts and braces thing again Heroes making sure you understand the consequences of your chosen position and the group.

You know 'the group' still wants to retain its power and control over you and from a survival perspective, 'the group' cares jack about the individual and its rights. Tell me how this understanding helps you today. Anyone?"

Tim: "We understand we are transitioning from childhood dependence on our family group for survival, to our peer group, aka our generation, for acceptance and support. Again, it's all about the group, its control and its conforming expectations. I'm social, I like to be out there, and I like the security, support and acceptance of belonging to a group. I give up my individual rights to belong to my peer group. I'm okay with that."

Max: "I can see why most people like the security of belonging to a group, but as Coach said in one our earlier sessions, "There's a catch! Handing the responsibility for our approval over to anyone or a group to feel okay about ourselves gives them all our power and puts us in a vulnerable position.

To be accepted and supported by the group, we must give up our individual power. That's the deal. Either way, there are consequences. If we choose not to belong to the group, we risk rejection, but we retain our power and our right as an individual to do our own thing. I know which I prefer."

Bethy: "I think it's about taking responsibility for our choices and being okay with the choices we make. To belong to the group and give up our power, or to risk rejection and choose independence and freedom. I know which I prefer too Max."

Grace: "I agree with Tim. I like security and the social component of belonging too. I feel supported by group acceptance, whether it's my peer group or my dance team, and I like approval. I know I have choices; I'm happy with my choice."

Queenie: "I agree with Max. I don't want to give the group all my power either. I like owning my independence. Realising there are consequences to my independent behaviour, sits okay with me too."

Coach: "It's a simple personal choice, when it's all boiled down, isn't it? All okay with your choices and their consequences, Heroes? Yes?

Okay. It's time to build you a 'rave review' self-image. We'll start with words and affirmations."

WORDS AND AFFIRMATIONS

Coach: "Most of us don't think about our self-image, do we? From my experience, few people have updated their self-image, which means most of us are thinking of ourselves through our inner child's self-image!

The aim of this exercise is to create an 'upbeat rave review' comparing who you are now to when you were a child. Like we did in Day 2, remember? when we compared childhood perspectives in the Childhood Model with your more grown-up interpretation.

Accepting your differences, that it's okay to be different and that none of us can be like anyone else, is a major lead up to liking yourself and to help you create a powerful up-to-date self-image.

You also know the Moon sign position in your Natal Chart and favourable career choices; choosing a career with an emotional connection is incredibly powerful!

To align with who you are today, write down, in dot point form, all the things that have advanced or changed since you were a child. For example, you have more responsibility now. Take a few minutes to jot them down:

....

....

....

....

....

Now we've set the comparison scene, I remind you of how your childhood image was formed:

No input into your childhood image:

Your inner child's feelings about himself and his identity, his sense of importance, self-esteem, value and self-worth were all formed from the feedback he was receiving by how others reacted to him."

Queenie: "So if we don't understand, or if we deny or we're unaware of the two-time zones, we continue living by our original inner child's image. My childhood image had me thinking I wasn't good enough or as good as the other kids. I disliked myself for that too."

Coach: "Yes, Queenie. Thank you. Positive or negative, your childhood image does impact your feelings about yourself, no doubt your career choices and your potential. So, our image needs updating aligned with who we are now, compared to a literal 7-year-old child.

Let's explore your internal dialogue. What words and phrases do you regularly use when talking to yourself? Do they criticise you, stunt your potential and keep you in your comfort zone, or are they uplifting and encouraging words and phrases that build your confidence? Without thinking, write down the words and phrases you use regularly on yourself.

....

....

....

....

....

Basically, what you are doing Heroes is disrupting automatic subconscious reactions i.e., old programs running in your head relating to your childhood self-image. Anyone with a comment?"

Queenie: "Me again... until this Course, I didn't realise how much I put myself down when I criticised myself. Thanks to Coach, I came to realise just how powerful words are and I've changed the way I talk to myself. I now use words that lift me up. I even praise myself! something I would never have done a week ago."

Coach: "Brilliant Queenie. I love these types of comparisons. Anyone else with a comment?"

Tim: "I feel the same. I didn't realise how damaging words can be on our psyche, self-esteem and self-worth. Also, how the words we say to ourselves can influence whether we like ourselves or not."

Coach: "Great insights Tim. Thank you. The words you use when talking to yourself have a big bearing on whether you like yourself or not. You're in charge of those words now. You have the power to change the way you view and feel about yourself.

What image-building words inspire you?

Highlight any words in your journal that resonate with you or inspire you:

powerful	passionate	intuitive
resourceful	reliable	diplomatic
decisive	optimistic	motivated

creative	assertive	responsible
imaginative	practical	courageous
empathic	adaptable	focused

Now take a few minutes to write down your special words; challenging words you can grow into, words that motivate and inspire you. If you have an idol, a role model or two, add their qualities to help you further:

....

....

....

....

....

Your attraction to each of your choices shows they already have their seeds in you. It's like admiring certain qualities in someone. Those qualities are within you too, waiting to be recognised and acknowledged.

This is exciting! The words you have chosen will give you a strong foundational base to work with. Use your chosen words to lift your spirits, and any time you're in a tough situation.

Now let's add a few personal affirmations you can use to build your confidence or when you're quietly talking to yourself. Who'd like to start?"

Bethy: "I'll start. Solitary time is important to me. I'm okay on my own."

Max: "Self-responsibility is awesome. I feel its power."

Grace: "I adapt to change easily."

Coach: "Oh! You really get the hang of this! Well done, Heroes! How about one each from Queenie and Tim."

Queenie: "I use my choices to empower my position."

Tim: "I'm bigger than this situation. I can do this!"

Coach: "Wow! I'm impressed! Great work and great understanding Heroes. There's a Handout with more powerful affirmations at the end of today's session. Lots to choose from. I know you'll love them.

Okay, let's take our 30-minute break now. While on your break, think about your new image. Project yourself into the future… what do you want your life to look like/to feel like in a year's time, two years' time, five years? What's your emotional connection to your career choice? Do you feel inspired? It's all ahead of you Heroes. Make it yours! I'll give you a set of questions on your return to help get you started. See you back here at quarter to."

YOUR UPDATED 'RAVE REVIEW' SELF-IMAGE

Coach: "Now let's pull it all together, building your confidence and new beliefs in yourself to take home, in tune with who you're aspiring to be.

You're in charge of your image now; project manage your life. See your life as something you are building, something you are creating, something to believe in... this is your new survival plan, thriving in your time zone in a modern world.

Think about your career choices, your Moon sign and your emotional connection with those career choices. Are you inspired? What's your passion? What do you want to build?

....

....

....

List ways you can work on your independence, taking self-responsibility and self-reliance to the next level:

....

....

....

Incorporate your chosen words into a sentence:

"I am ....

...."

Now add your affirmation/s:

"
....
"

"
....
"

"
....
"

Where would you like to be in one year, two years, even five years from now? What would this feel like/look like to you? Short-term, medium and long-term visions will help you stay focused.

One year:

....

....

....

Two years:

....

....

....

Five years:

....

....

....

Play with a Courage Shopping List:

Do you want to ask someone out on a date? Do you want to ask for assistance? Do you want to apply for a casual job? You get the idea... something that needs your courage.

....

....

....

Okay Heroes, you've done the groundwork. Your homework tonight will be to read the Affirmations Handout, choose the affirmations that most resonate with you and complete your updated self-image. When you get home, keep your 'rave review' self-image on your Vision Board or in your scrap book. If you have any questions after the Course, please let me know.

Just a reminder, you will always be a work in progress. Keeping your image updated will invite all kinds of wonderful things into your life and the courage to go after them, *even if you feel like an imposter every time!* Action brings your power to life and acting the part will build your confidence and a new belief in yourself. Let's add more power to your arsenal."

MORE PERSONAL POWER

Coach: "We've all heard of Journalling, right? Who'd like to explain why they keep a journal?"

KEEPING A JOURNAL:

Bethy: "Keeping a private journal or a diary is a great way to get to know yourself, staying in tune with your feelings, aspirations and your goals. You can record your day-to-day or week-to-week achievements and activities, anything that worries you, solutions to your problems etc. basically keeping track of your progress."

Coach: "Excellent explanation Bethy. Thank you. Now, has anyone heard of a Vision Board?"

A VISION BOARD:

Grace: "It's a picture board you pin motivational things on to inspire you."

Coach: "Yes, Grace. Thank you. It's a picture board, a visual, of everything that motivates, inspires and encourages you. It could contain affirmations, like we've just discussed, it could also include photos, expressions, pictures, magazine articles, books you'd like to read. Its main purpose is to help you stay motivated and connected to your goals and aspirations.

Vision boards come in different sizes. If you don't have the space, or there's little privacy at home, a scrap book would be a great alternative."

Queenie: "You could easily change the content of your Vision Board or scrap book as your goals change or as you move forward, couldn't you?"

Coach: "Yes Queenie. Staying up to date with your goals, visions, your motivations is a good point. Anyone willing to work with a Vision Board or a scrap book?"

Heroes in unison: "Yes. Great idea Coach."

Coach: "Let's talk about money. Who has a casual job?"

MONEY:

Queenie: "I have a casual job on weekends working in an art and craft store."

Max: "My band plays at different venues including pubs and 21st birthday parties. It's good fun and we get paid."

Coach: "Great. What does it *feel* like to earn your own money?"

Queenie: "It feels empowering Coach. I don't have to ask my parents for money for everything. It gives me a sense of privacy too. I feel good when I'm a bit independent."

Max: "Yeah! I like the independence too. It aligns with my sense of self-responsibility. It gives me a sense of power and dignity too; helps me to feel good about myself."

Coach: "Anyone else with a casual job? No? That's okay. I mention it because it's amazing how good the human spirit feels when we are earning even small amounts of money through our own endeavours; it's incredibly satisfying and rewarding. Not relying on anyone for your everyday needs is wonderfully empowering too. It's one of the secrets to a happy life. It has a huge positive impact on your sense of worth and self-esteem too.

Successful men and women thrive on their inner knowledge that they are resourceful, independent and self-sufficient. Independence both emotionally and financially are great power brokers.

Some of my past students' casual jobs have led to traineeships for management positions within those organisations.

Still on money, have you heard of Scott Pape's 'The Barefoot Investor'?"

Tim: "Yes, I have. It's a #1Australian bestseller on personal finances."

Coach: "Yes, Tim. Thank you. It's brilliant and original. Basically, written for young people. They say the only money guide you'll ever need. Practical advice for achieving financial independence and security. Eliminating debt and building wealth. Highly recommended reading and reference. The classic printed edition of 'The Barefoot Investor' was published by Wiley, 2022. There is also a 3-part documentary series… same title.

Now here's something you may not have heard of:

THE HIGHLY SENSITIVE PERSON (HSP):

This is one category of people who feel profoundly 'different'. Twenty percent of the population are highly sensitive. That's one in five people. There is almost certainly one person in this room who fits into the HSP category. These people are wonderfully different. I have included a Handout on Highly Sensitive People. There's also a couple of books I recommend if you identify with this personality type.

Okay, let's touch on a familiar topic:

SELF-RESPONSIBILITY:

I know we've covered this topic in previous sessions, but self-responsibility is the first step towards owning and feeling your power. What's our Course #1 affirmation Heroes? Say it like you mean it...

Heroes shouting: *"It's good to feel my power and it's great to own my power."*

Coach: "Roger that! Self-responsibility increases our self-esteem and self-worth and positively impacts our self-image. It's the difference between no responsibility and the total dependence of your inner child, and you today making positive strides towards independence and taking tiny steps towards caring for yourself. There is nothing like self-reliance to boost your confidence.

How do you take on self-responsibility?

You become accountable for what is happening in your life. You decide to step up and take over childhood powerlessness. They are your choices in action. For example, you can decide to:

- get to classes on time

- do your homework without being reminded

- keep your room reasonably tidy

- live up to your promises, especially those you make to yourself.

- decide whether you want to belong to a group, but aware of the consequences.

Who can think of any others?"

Tim: "In my case, it's about having a sincere discussion with my parents about my career choices."

Coach: "Oh! Tim. That's a big action. A big heroes cheer for Tim."

Heroes cheering: "Hooray for Tim!" ☺☺☺☺☺

Coach: "Anyone else?"

Queenie: "Be mindful of how I'm speaking to myself. Encourage myself with empowering words and positive affirmations to lift my confidence."

Max: "Taking ownership for how social I want to be. I'll let my teachers know I'm okay with my choice when they start riding me to join in more. I'll never forget: the group cares jack about me; it just wants me to comply. Thanks Coach."

Bethy: "Find a casual job. It will take some of the financial pressure off my mum too."

Coach: "Oh! All excellent forms of self-responsibility. How about you Grace? Any thoughts?"

Grace: "Let my teachers know that I'm capable of dancing and achieving academic excellence when I choose my career path."

Coach: "Ooh! That's another big one! Excellent Grace! Taking responsibility for your choices. Trust me: when you start relying on yourself, baby steps first, there'll be no going back to your inner child's dependence on others. It's huge!"

Has anyone heard the expression: *"How do you eat an elephant?"*

Heroes laughing: "No Coach."

Coach: "The elephant is your challenge. How do you eat an elephant? One bite at a time! It means taking small steps Heroes.

Now more on career choices. Remember not everyone needs a tertiary qualification. In fact, some 'unqualified' success stories reach billionaire status. We've already mentioned Steve Jobs. Another perfect example of 'unqualified' is Richard Branson. He left school at 16! He considers life to be a long educational experience. Have you heard of Richard Branson?"

Heroes: "Yes Coach. He started Virgin Airlines."

Coach: "He sure did! How many times was he told, "that's not possible!" And he did it anyway... and now he's *Sir* Richard Branson! Creating Virgin Airlines is an example of "that's not possible" turned into "watch me achieve the impossible"! Amazing vision, dedication and persistence, and oh! his passion.

To balance the ledger, here's one lady who had a tertiary education and has achieved billionaire status, J.K. Rowling. You all know who she is, right."

Heroes in unison: "She wrote the Harry Potter books."

Coach: "Yes, indeed! J.K. Rowling wrote the Harry Potter series of books. She attended the University of Exeter where she studied French and Classics, earning her degree in 1986.

Just pointing out, Heroes, education is important, but not everyone goes down the same path to achieve their goal. No right or wrong here... all about the individual and choices.

YOUR CAREER CHOICE:

A little deeper on this subject now. Choose your career – your subject – something you love to do or something that piques your curiosity or intrigue… something that is bigger than you. A service to others. Learn your craft deeply and take your time – there are no shortcuts and no enduring fast money. Passion, persistence and dedication win!

As I discovered, the deeper my knowledge on one subject, the more insights, revelations and light bulb moments were channelled to me. Go deep, then go deeper; become the specialist, the guru, the expert in your chosen endeavour. There is a but… with all the fast changes today, careers can change quickly and become obsolete so always keep up with what is happening around you. Did bells ring for anyone?"

Grace: "That was so motivational Coach. *Something bigger than you. A service to others.* I'll never forget your words."

Tim: "Yeah! I liked, *passion, persistence and dedication win!*"

Max: "Becoming *a specialist, a guru, an expert* did it for me. Thanks Coach."

Coach: "You're very welcome. Any thoughts Queenie and Bethy?"

Queenie: "Yes. Specialist on one subject appeals to me too and there's *no shortcuts and no such thing as enduring fast money.*"

Bethy: "I like *"go deep, then go deeper."* Thanks Coach."

Coach: "Thank you Heroes. I'm pleased you all got something from my little speech. Can you handle a few more tips?"

COURAGE... PERSONAL SUCCESS

Heroes: "Yes, Coach."

Coach: "Okay:

- Devote time to your physical fitness. Stay well.

- Choose a way of expressing yourself emotionally.

- Stay on top of things… the longer you allow a situation to fester, the bigger and more unmanageable it becomes and the more power it has over you. Nip it in the bud!

- You are the game-changer of your life. No-one can do this for you.

- No-one in your peer group owns you! and no-one in a romantic relationship owns you either!

- You are your own best friend, and you have the power to decide what is in your best interests.

- Walking away is your courage and ultimate power.

Any questions? No? Okay Heroes, time to wrap up our *'Making Friends'* Course. I want you to know, I have enjoyed every minute getting to know you and working with you. My hope is that you'll form your own Heroes' Club. Most of my Course Heroes remain great friends years later, encouraging each other to live bigger lives.

Please update me by email; you have my address. Tell me what career paths you will be taking and any other news you'd like to share with me. I look forward to reading any reviews you post for this Course too. I can't wait to read your email updates.

161

Congratulations on being my Course Heroes. Don't forget to take a copy of the four Handouts on the desk near the door.

Max on behalf of the Heroes: "Coach, I speak on our behalf. We are not the same people we were five days ago! Thank you for passing on life's wisdom. We are all inspired to be of service to others, to build and to make something of ourselves…. we're gonna miss you Coach! We made a pact to enrol in your *'Mastering the mechanics of your life'* Course in 20 years."

Coach: holding back an emotional response. "Wow! Thank you. This is a first – enrolling in *'The Mastering Course'*. I look forward to welcoming you to that course too. I'll have to figure out in the meantime, how everyone will fit into my Mustang V8 fastback coupe to do that Course! ☺ I'm going to miss you too my Heroes. Be true to yourself; stay safe. Enjoy the rest of your summer holiday."

HEROES' NOTES

....

....

....

....

....

....

....

....

....

....

....

....

....

....

....

....

....

....

....

HANDOUTS

HANDOUT 1: AFFIRMATIONS

The power of affirmations cannot be underestimated. They can lift you up when you need encouragement; boost your confidence and praise your efforts. They can be likened to a life coach:

- **"I am enough. I am okay."**

- "I love the feeling of self-responsibility."

- "Passion, persistence and dedication win."

- **"I am a winner!"**

- "I am no longer a child. I can do this!"

- "I am in a major transitional phase. I am okay."

- **"This is a phase in my life. I'll get through this. I will be okay."**

- **"Nothing lasts. Everything changes. I am okay."**

- "Feelings change."

- **"I am okay with or without the approval of others."**

- "I am proud of everything I am achieving today."

- **"I know how the survival system works. I am okay without group approval."**

- "I'm not like anyone else on this planet! I am okay being me."

- "I love feeling empowered. I follow up on promises I make to myself."

- **"I am my own best friend. I love being me."**

- "I don't quit. I am not a quitter. I will get through this."

- **"I have the courage to walk away when I feel pressured."**

- **"I'm in charge of life-or-death decisions. I choose life every time."**

- "Choices add to my empowerment."

- **"Conformity sucks the power from my life."**

- "Fear is my personal bodyguard. It helps me survive."

- **"Rejection is a consequence if I don't conform. THAT'S ALL IT IS. I am not a victim."**

- "I acknowledge the presence and wisdom of anger. I give it space to vent. Anger is my emotional bodyguard. It wants the best for me."

- "I update my inner child's beliefs about me."

- **"I compliment and praise myself often."**

- "I cut myself some slack. Perfection doesn't exist in the real world."

- **"Different is okay. I am gentle on myself."**

- "I question all the shoulds and have tos in my life."

- **"It's okay to fail. I am closer to success."**

- **"I choose to be responsible, self-reliant and empowered. They are my choices."**

- "I give myself a big hug when things get rough."

- **"Life is tough; I was born tougher. I'll get through this! I am okay."**

- "I change my inner child's, '*I can't do this*' to '*I'll try!*' It's my choice."

- "Standing up for myself gets easier with practice."

- **"I have big plans for me and my life. Watch this space..."**

- "I feel safe and supported. I have many layers of support."

Your turn. Add your favourites here:

....

....

....

HANDOUT 2: THE HIGHLY SENSITIVE PERSON

Highly sensitive people represent 20% of the population; one in five people are highly sensitive. They operate from a different emotional base.

Your highly sensitive nature and your deeper intensity may not have been recognised or may have been mismanaged or misinterpreted when you were a child. Your differences are now being recognised, respected and appreciated. You should give yourself special consideration too.

The characteristics of Highly Sensitive People (HSPs) are:

- You feel deeper with more intensity

- You tire more easily

- You become deeply involved in things that matter to you

- You are overly trusting

- You take a lot longer to get over betrayal

- You can be exploited more easily

- You feel a need to explain or justify yourself

- You often find life overwhelming

- You need more alone time

- You are slower to get things because you go deeper and have a need to understand deeply

- Your spirit can be affected by staying too long in a job of drudgery or in an inflexible routine

- You are among the most creative people in the world.

Did you connect with any of the above characteristics?

....

....

....

Why is a HSP seen as 'different'?

- You are basically a loner

- You are very sensitive, intense and serious

- You can be misinterpreted – seen as shy or sometimes antisocial

- You don't fit in easily

- You may appear clumsy and awkward

- You are a perfectionist

- You can't do half a job – it's all or nothing for you

- You are totally ethical.

If you think you are a 1 in 5, take heart. You will continue to discover a never-ending stream of untapped talents. As you embrace all your talents and continue to reinvent yourself, you will evolve.

Your career becomes a search. You are looking for real meaning in your life. You have a calling to excel.

Your special gifts also have special needs:

You are often multi-talented with deep intelligence and imagination, but because you are more likely to stand on the sidelines rather than join in, you can be mistakenly seen as introverted or aloof. You see others as forthright, out there enjoying themselves with a strength you feel is missing from your life. This leads to deeper feelings of overwhelm, ineffectiveness and not fitting in anywhere.

Your biggest lesson is to learn to trust your feelings.

Accepting your differences is a major lead up to liking yourself. Have the courage to go deeper, to investigate and discover your real personality and emotional nature. Astrology will be immensely helpful.

From one HSP to another, here's a couple of books I recommend:

- Aron, E. (2003), *The Highly Sensitive Person: How to Thrive When the World Overwhelms You*, Thorsons/Element, Great Britain.

- Jaeger, B. (2005), *Making Work Work for the Highly Sensitive Person*, McGraw-Hill Education, U.S.A.

HANDOUT 3: TRIBAL BELIEFS, ATTITUDES & BEHAVIOURS

Think about the beliefs, attitudes/biases, and behaviours, frequently displayed by your tribal family. Just like caveman children, we copy them, and they become generational cycles mindlessly repeating themselves as fast, subconscious, automatic reactions... like your reaction to astrology.

Can you identify any of your tribal family's beliefs, attitudes/ biases and behaviours? List them.

....

....

....

....

....

Are they working in your best interests today? Any you'd like to review?

....

....

....

....

....

HANDOUT 4: A TRIBUTE TO YOUR INNER CHILD

"I love my inner child's primal simplicity –
Her beliefs in the first seven years created our history.
My inner child believes she is all she can be…
She is the younger version of me.

I see everything through my inner child's eyes…
Her beliefs become my beliefs until I am wise.
She is dependent and powerless in every way –
I show her there's more when I shoo fear away.

With her by my side I make perfect sense…
She is the substance, the heart and the core of my essence.
Our 'dream team' consciousness transforms my identity.
I am complete and transcending my inner child's destiny."

Louise L. Kallaway.

HEROES' EMAILS TO COACH

FROM GRACE:

Dear Coach,

I hope you're busy enlightening more Heroes. It's been a couple of busy months since I finished the *'Making Friends with Yourself'* Course. As promised, I'm writing to bring you up to date.

Remember I felt pressure from my teachers to choose a career path? I made the decision that whatever career I chose, it could never be boring or routine. It had to be in line with my Aries Moon sign or I would lose interest very quickly. I have a competitive spirit, I'm social and I love motivational speaking; my role model is Arnold Schwarzenegger.

I've decided to study a Master of Marketing and Digital Communications. This online globally accepted degree prepares its students to influence at the highest level across business, government and the community. I thought I could establish a social media presence on Meta (Facebook) and a following on LinkedIn so people who were interested, may be even a few businesses, could come along for the ride as I do my degree. I could offer services during my degree to help businesses and sole practitioners, making it easier on my parents financially too.

My goal will be motivational speaking whether its public speaking or in a teaching capacity. I know I'm aiming high Coach, but if I miss the (Aries) moon, I'll land among the stars. I read something like that somewhere. ☺ In Day 2 of the '*Making Friends*' Course, I said I wanted something to believe in. Now I have!

Thank you, Coach. Without knowing my Moon sign, I doubt I would have found my way so quickly. I'm happy to tell you, my teachers are all behind me now that I have a direction. I still love the team spirit of competition dancing and have no thought of giving it up.

I stay in touch with everyone, Coach, especially Queenie. It will be fun to see where we all end up.

I wish you super success with your courses and your franchising, Coach. '*Making Friends with Yourself*' made a big impact on me; it's the best course for young people who want to understand this transitional stage and how to make a bigger life for themselves.

Best wishes to you and your life-changing work Coach.

Your friend, Grace.

P.S. I'll post my 5-Star review when I'm happy with it.

EMAIL FROM TIM:

Hi there Coach,

I recently read your *'Making Friends with Yourself'* course broke even more franchising records! Congratulations! I hope you liked my 5-star review.

I tell everyone especially my peer group about your course and if they can, they should enrol in the *'Making Friends'* course to be smarter and wiser. ☺

When I got home from Summer School, I debriefed my parents about your course and then I pre-empted the conversation about my career choice by explaining that my love of basketball and my passion for coaching had already planted the seeds. They immediately saw the connection.

As you know, I was very concerned about my parent's reaction. I thought I would have to use my emotional courage a lot more, but my parents were surprisingly supportive when I explained I wanted to eventually run my own business as a One Stop Sports Clinic. It would include a gym, personal trainers, a dietician, a physio, a sports psychologist and eventually other professions that fitted in with those disciplines. I then mentioned I would like to study physiotherapy. I would become a Personal trainer first to help with the finances and then study physiotherapy part time as the business was being established. Pisces moon people are very intuitive, as you know, so wanting to provide a service and intuitively being guided, feels perfect. Thanks Coach.

My parents run a very successful sales and marketing business; they want to be part of my dream and help turn it into a reality. I don't know who is more excited, them or me! They can already see my Clinic excelling!

LOUISE L. KALLAWAY

I stay in touch with everyone who was in the course, especially Max who is my Hero. One day I will watch him on stage.

I can't thank you enough Coach. Please let me know if I can do anything for you.

Cheers!

Tim.

EMAIL FROM QUEENIE:

Hello Coach.

It's great to be writing to you Coach. I wanted to say, at least one more time, how much your *'Making Friends with Yourself'* course has meant to me. Without it, who knows where I'd be, especially when I was thinking I wasn't as good as the other kids. I owe you Coach. ☺

Regarding my career, I kept thinking about what you said, *"when your heart is in your career choice, you'll never work another day."* I love beautiful things, drawing and colour and my Taurus moon appreciates beauty and building something. I'm fascinated by Interior Design and Decorating and their amazing transformations and as you know, Laura Ashley and the late Stuart Rattle are my role models.

Meeting with private clients, architects and builders and working on my own developing designs and concepts for them, gives me that balance I need between time with clients and time on my own. It's perfect Coach. I'm so excited. I *feel* this is my calling!

On other news, Grace and I email each other with updates. We also asked Bethy if she'd like to stay in touch. She said, "Yes!"

Thank you, Coach. I'll never forget you, your Course and the new life-long friendships I made there.

Sincere regards,

Queenie.

P.S. I hope you liked my review. I meant every word.

EMAIL FROM MAX:

Gooday Coach.

Still messing with young people's heads? ☺ I hope so Coach – your course changed my life... forever. I posted a 5-star review for *'Making Friends with Yourself'* on Google. Let me know if I can do more Coach.

Regarding my career choice: You've given me so much to work with. I'll never forget my kneejerk reaction to astrology. A life lesson. Thanks Coach.

As you know, I resonate with my age group; I'm seriously thinking of becoming a Youth Worker, maybe teaching your *'Making Friends with yourself'* Course too, remember? I also see myself running some sort of boot camp for young people who don't fit it, giving them hope for their future. I really connect with that idea too.

I discovered there is a Bachelor of Youth Work degree that focusses on supporting and empowering young people. It provides a foundation in youth development, social justice, community engagement, equipping graduates with the skills and knowledge they need in various settings. What I really like about the degree is that graduates develop skills in not only program planning and facilitation, but it covers my Libran Moon natural mediator tendencies towards counselling, conflict resolution and leadership. It *feels* like a great fit Coach. I think this course will balance my independence and social needs nicely too. Getting the balance right is when my heart sings.

My Heavy Metal band is getting plenty of work and we are still coming up with great music and lyrics. I love the harmony and the respect within the band and the public.

You probably know already, but we all stay in touch, and we're all excited about our prospects. Your *'Making Friends'* course has been an incredible life-changing experience for all of us.

Thanks for your extra time, Coach, explaining how I can become one of your franchisees. Stay fit and well. I'd like to stay in touch.

Best regards,

Max.

EMAIL FROM BETHY:

Hello Coach.

I miss our conversations! My mum says one of the best things she did was enrol me in your *'Making Friends with Yourself'* course. I stay in touch with the other students too! She can't believe the 'before and after the course' differences with me and my new casual job! ☺ That's right! Thanks Coach.

Regarding my career: I have a Scorpio moon. I think psychology is a good fit. I know you thought psychology would be a great choice for me too, especially with my love of research and deep investigation. Lately, I've been thinking I could write stories about my research making them real with life-like characters. A magic fit for me too. The big picture presents many diverse opportunities; while I'm studying, I could stay with my mum because Psychology is one of the degrees taught at my local university.

Remember when I said, maybe I could get some work to help my mum financially? I decided to enquire about casual work with the huge library at the same local University. It happened they were short staffed and offered me a job three days a week after school putting books back onto shelves! I couldn't believe my luck. Thanks Coach.

I continue my love of writing short stories; maybe one day I'll assemble them, include a few tales about people's kryptonite, and publish a book. Do you remember that I chose my mum as my #1 role model, but after hearing the others' nominations, I decided I was only halfway?

Once I made the decision to become a psychologist, I did some research to find a role model in psychology, and I came across the late, Dr. Wayne Dyer (1940-2015). Did you know his famous book, *"Your Erroneous Zones"* was rejected by many publishers at the time? He believed in his work, and he believed in himself, so he mortgaged his house and put the proceeds into publishing his book. He drove across America, dropping the books into libraries and bookshops, signing his book and giving talks along the way. By the time he arrived in New York City, two years later, word of mouth about his book was out there and lots of interviews were waiting for him. Turns out, America was ready for his new-age psychological book after all! He inspires me; the late Dr. Wayne Dyer is my #3 Hero.

Thanks again Coach. I couldn't be where I am today without you and your *'Making Friends with Yourself'* Course. You are my greatest influencer and my #2 Hero.

Best wishes, Coach.

Bethy.

P.S. I'm still dotting the i's on my 5-star review. I'll post it soon Coach.

THANK YOU TO MY READERS

Coach: "Every once in a while, we come across an opportunity that can change our lives. Did you take up the offer? Did you read *'Courage''* from cover to cover and do the exercises with the other Heroes? Are you willing to make a bigger, more inspired life for yourself?

Do you feel safer after reading *'Courage'*? Feeling safe is one of the most coveted feelings in our lives from babies all the way through to old age. We all need to feel safe and supported to not only survive, but to thrive.

You are now awake to the system we were all born into that demands you fit in and conform to survive! You decide whether you want to, don't want to, can't or won't fit in and conform. It's up to you and remember, choices have consequences, and it will take courage to act on those choices. You are the powerful one now.

I hope *'Courage'* showed you how different we all are; that you can't be like anyone else and they can't be like you. You're in charge of your life... whether you want to belong to the group or not, is up to you. We all need support. **Support, especially at your age, is important.** Maybe, like Grace and Tim, belonging to the group feels okay for you. Maybe, you're more like Queenie and Max, and your attitude is 'take it or leave it' depending on what your peer group is expecting of you. Are you most like Bethy, who prefers her own company, and not conforming with the group? **Remember: it's your choice and taking responsibility for that choice makes you a winner!**

How do you feel about 'the group' now? Belonging to a group is part of our survival programming. The Universe gave survival power to the group. From a survival perspective, the group cares jack about the individual. If your peer group is threatening you or demanding you conform with its bullying-style behaviour, excluding you or making you feel like an outsider, then that group is not the right one for you. You are much more deserving! You don't need to put up with their behaviour! What would our Heroes do? They would have the courage to walk away.

Is there another group more aligned with your interests, such as a sports team or a computer club? Belonging to a group that has the same interests as you, could be a much better fit. Whichever group you choose, remember it will have rules, and it will expect you to conform.

Do you need to belong to a group? Maybe you feel supported, like Bethy, by a parent or like Queenie with her grand mum. Do you have a confidant? someone who will listen to you, or help you with your feelings? If not, for everyone who lives in Australia, you can phone any of the following 24/7 services:

Headspace: 1800 650 890

Lifeline: 13 11 14 or text 0477 131 114

Beyond Blue: 1300 22 4636

Suicide Callback service: 1300 659 467

Kids Helpline: 1800 55 1800

COURAGE... THANK YOU TO MY READERS

Don't delay, phone today! Admitting to how you feel and talking to someone to help sort out your feelings is heroic. Power to you and the little kid in you. Always know, you are not alone... you have layers of support.

To all young people not living in Australia, please check Google and your local support organisations.

Will you take time out to watch the highly recommended movie, *'Goodwill Hunting'*? Will you read *'Jonathan Livingston Seagull'*, ASAP, and find time to read *'The Warrior Within'* and *'The Barefoot Investor'*? If you are a *Highly Sensitive Person*, there are a couple of books I recommend that can help make your life easier too. All great reading when you need a boost, Hero. ☺

Did you enjoy reading our Heroes emails to Coach? Do you know your Moon sign? Remember, when you are connected emotionally to your career you'll never work a day in your life. What will your career choice be?

You have made new friends and joined the Heroes in this book. You are part of this special support group. Use *'Courage''* as your guide, a reference, whenever you need it. The Enid Blyton *'Famous Five'* detective stories were my special 'go to' books. Whenever I needed company, I would open one of those books. I had my favourites among the 'Famous Five' detectives too. Do you have a favourite or favourites in *'Courage'*?

"It's good to feel my power and its great to own my power."

Did you build a new 'rave review' self-image? Will you set up a Vision board or a scrap book, maybe start a journal to help track your progress? Find yourself a casual job?

Congratulations on getting to the end of this book! You are a Winner already! Give yourself permission to live the life you envision for yourself. Your chosen idol and/or role model/s can help you do this. Continue conquering the things you write on your courage shopping list. ☺

I wish you every success, my Hero. What will you do with your gift of life, I wonder."

ABOUT COACH

I started writing my 'Life Education' books, in 2012, assembling 30 years of my research into book and journal form. My first six books were written as classic author to reader. Then, came an idea, thanks Trish! to write my research as realistic fiction and non-fiction novels. It was easier to understand my life's work in a classroom kind of situation and the impact on the individual in the 21st Century.

I love writing in the new realistic fiction style, or non-fiction novel style, a kind of script writing, making sense of people's lives. Getting into each of the personalities that are the heroes in my books, so you can relate to those characters and share their different viewpoints is exciting. Beaming powerful light on the power of the group and why independence and personal power has been so difficult for most of us to achieve, until now, is inspiring to me.

May '*Courage*' become a classic read for teenagers and young people globally and find its way into secondary colleges, book clubs, libraries and universities… everywhere young people congregate.

If you can help distribute this book, please contact me via my website: louiselkallaway@louiselkallaway.com

TITLES IN THE 'LIFE EDUCATION' BOOKS & JOURNALS

- EMPOWERED. Secrets of your inner child.

- DEFIANCE. Secrets of your midlife crisis.

- EVOLVING. Secrets of a child and life processes.

- You and your inner child today journal.

- CONSCIOUS. 'How life works' journal.

- SURVIVAL. 'How fear works' journal.

- ONCE UPON A T!ME… How life's story becomes your story.

- T!ME… How life's story became your story.

- WINNING. The fight for your Life.

www.ingramcontent.com/pod-product-compliance
Lightning Source LLC
Chambersburg PA
CBHW050841270326
41930CB00019B/3424